MW00614540

# BASIC
# TRAINING
## FOR
# PROPHETIC
# ACTIVATION

# BASIC TRAINING

# FOR

# PROPHETIC

# ACTIVATION

DAN McCOLLAM

© Copyright 2012—Dan McCollam

All rights reserved. This book is protected by the copyright laws of the United States of America. This book may not be copied or reprinted for commercial gain or profit. The use of short quotations or occasional page copying for personal or group study is permitted. Permission will be granted upon request.

Unless otherwise identified, Scripture quotations are taken from the HOLY BIBLE, NEW INTERNATIONAL VERSION®. Copyright © 1973, 1978, 1984 International Bible Society. Used by permission of Zondervan. All rights reserved.

Scripture quotations are taken from the HOLY BIBLE, THE NEW AMERICAN STANDARD BIBLE (NASB)®. Copyright © 1960, 1962, 1963, 1968, 1971, 1972, 1973, 1975, 1977, 1995 by The Lockman Foundation, La Habra, CA. All rights reserved. Used by permission. (www. Lockman.org).

PUBLISHED BY:

iWAR (Institute of Worship Arts Resources) and SOUNDS OF THE NATIONS

6391 Leisure Town Road, Vacaville, California 95687

COVER DESIGN & PHOTOGRAPHY BY:  Jared Teska

Teska Photography & Design

JaredTeskaPhotography.com

Printed in the United States of America

First Edition: July 2012

ISBN-10: 098518633X

ISBN-13: 978-0-9851863-3-3

# CONTENTS

The prophetic is meant
to be a divine dialogue with the
Holy Spirit.

# FOREWORD

have known Dano McCollam for more than 14 years. Together we have trained and equipped thousands of people in both the office of the prophet and the gift of prophecy. Dano is one of the wisest and most insightful people I've ever had the privilege of knowing. His amazing relationship with God and his incredible insight into the Word are hallmarks of his life and ministry. Dano has so assimilated God's Word into his own life that it has become cellular in him, like a beautiful celestial union between the message and the messenger! This gives him the unique ability to take complicated concepts and make them simple and applicable to everyday life.

*Basic Training for Prophetic Activation* is the right word in the right season because this outpouring has inspired an insatiable hunger for the gift of prophecy among so many believers. The apostle Peter said in the last days God would pour His Spirit out on all flesh. The predominant manifestation of this heavy rain is the gift of prophecy being distributed to every person regardless of his or her age, gender, or social class. The great apostle Paul put it this way, "earnestly desire spiritual gifts but especially that you would prophesy." Prophetic conferences are taking place in record numbers all over the world. Several new prophetic books are released every month as leaders around the globe labor to teach and equip Christians in the mists of this spiritual downpour.

Most conferences, schools, and books teach believers the theological and philosophical foundations that need to be laid in our hearts so that we can live a healthy supernatural life. There is very little being taught, however, about how to practically activate and evaluate the prophetic gift in an individual's life.

I love Dano McCollam's new book *Basic Training for Prophetic Activation* because it fills a much-needed void in the practical application of the prophetic ministry. In this powerful book Dano unearths several simple tools that will unlock hidden treasures and secret mysteries that have eluded our perception and reduced our revelation. This book is full of practical insights—the prophetic nature of a name, how your five senses can be activated by the Holy Spirit to receive heavenly insight, how to bring people into the Kingdom with the gift of prophecy, and much more.

Whether you are a brand new believer or a seasoned prophetic warrior, this book is for you. You will be inspired, encouraged, challenged, and equipped to join this revolution. It is time to deploy a massive army of radical revivalists to the darkest places of the planet to bring light and hope to a desperate and despairing world. Your destiny is in need of you!

—Kris Vallotton
Leader, Bethel Church, Redding, California
Cofounder of Bethel School of Supernatural Ministry
Author of eight books including *The Supernatural Ways of Royalty*
and *Spirit Wars.*

God has a dream:
"Your sons and daughters will prophesy."

# INTRODUCTION

God has a dream. God dreams of a day when not only would there be prophets and prophetesses, but every son and daughter on earth would have the supernatural grace to perceive His heart and His voice in prophecy. He stated His dream this way:

*And afterward, I will pour out my Spirit on all people. Your sons and daughters will prophesy, your old men will dream dreams, your young men will see visions (Joel 2:28).*

*This is what was spoken by the prophet Joel: "In the last days, God says, I will pour out my Spirit on all people. Your sons and daughters will prophesy, your young men will see visions, your old men will dream dreams" (Acts 2:16-17).*

God made His own dream possible by paying the price for sin on the cross and crucifying the sin nature through Jesus Christ. He not only offered us His death but also partnership in His resurrection. By ascending to the very throne of God, Jesus was glorified and sent the Holy Spirit to fill man with the very same thing that fills God Himself. He initiated stage one of His dream by pouring out His Spirit on all flesh on the day of Pentecost.[1] Now all people—"all flesh"—can access the heart, the mind, and the intent of God through the prophetic gift and grace that has been lavishly poured out by the Holy Spirit.

The fact that this dream is still very much alive is best expressed in First Corinthians.

> *Follow the way of love and eagerly desire spiritual gifts, especially the gift of prophecy.*

> *But everyone who prophesies speaks to men for their strengthening, encouragement and comfort.*

> *I would like every one of you to speak in tongues, but I would rather have you prophesy* (14:1, 3, 5).

## The Prophetic Movement Sweeping the Earth

The Azusa Street Revival that began in Los Angeles, California, in 1906 brought the gift of speaking in tongues back into prominent usage in America and around the world. The Charismatic Movement of the early 1960s to late 1970s awakened this gift across historic mainstream congregations. It seemed like there were no longer small pockets of revival, but that truly His Spirit was being poured out on all people.

These Pentecostal and Charismatic movements have had such a

---

1   See Acts 2.

transformational effect upon society that in a special millennium[2] addition of *TIME Magazine,* the periodical listed The Azusa Street Revival as one of the top one hundred most important events in American history.

These awakenings of the 20th century were the beginnings of a modern fulfillment of God's dream spoken by the Prophet Joel and echoed in the writings of Paul. Paul said that he "would like every one of you to speak in tongues, but I would rather have you prophesy."[3]

The Pentecostal and Charismatic outpourings represent the blessings, grace, promise, and transformational impact of the first part of this verse. But what about the second part of this verse? If speaking in tongues changed the world in the 20th century, what will happen in the 21st century as we pursue Paul's preference and God's dream that all people would prophesy? Our potential to build others up in the Spirit, to pour courage into hearts, and to bring comfort to the world will be unparalleled in history through the current outpouring of prophetic grace.

## Activating Prophetic Grace

That is why it is so important that individuals and groups prepare themselves to activate and appropriate prophetic grace. This workbook is designed to help you with that task.

How do you begin to move in prophetic grace?

### First, you must earnestly desire to prophesy.

*Earnestly desire spiritual gifts, but especially that you may prophesy* (1 Corinthians 14:1, NASB).

---

2   Year 2000.
3   1 Corinthians 14:5 (NIV).

Don't just embrace that this gift is for today; believe that the prophetic gift and grace is for *you* personally. Desire it. Dream about giving others powerful, accurate, prophetic encouragement. Some would say, "I don't know if this gift is for me" or "I am not very prophetic."

Remember God's dream—that every son and daughter would prophesy. God made that dream possible for *you* by pouring out His Spirit on *all* people. Do not in any way disqualify yourself. Embrace the grace that is yours through the sacrifice of Christ and the outpouring of the Holy Spirit. Instead, say to yourself: "I was created for this. This is my gift. This is my grace. I was made to prophesy."

## Break ties with any past negative connections with the prophetic.

*Do not treat prophecies with contempt* (1 Thessalonians 5:20).

Many people share that they have had a bad experience with those who have mishandled prophetic grace. Others have heard stories of believers being manipulated into marrying the wrong person, quitting a good job, or giving away their life savings through false prophetic guidance. You may have even grown up in a religious tradition that taught that these gifts were no longer for today, and anyone who practices these gifts is moving by the power of the devil. Thoughts like these, along with feelings of spiritual inadequacy, can leave us with contempt for prophecy. You must break ties with those doubts, fears, and hurts.

Mistakes have indeed been made in the Body of Christ, both through wrong practice and wrong theology. Nevertheless, it is time to forgive. It is time to heal. It is time to move on in our own God-given destiny. Don't let the mistakes of others hold you back from being part of God's dream.

If you have had negative connections with prophecy, break them right now through repentance, forgiveness, and declarations of personal faith.

## Ask for, believe, and receive the gift of prophecy.

*For everyone who asks receives...(Luke 11:10).*

You may ask, *how do I know I will receive?* Be confident in God's Word which promises that everyone who asks will receive. Let's expand the above verse from Luke.

> *For everyone who asks receives; he who seeks finds; and to him who knocks, the door will be opened. Which of you fathers, if your son asks for a fish, will give him a snake instead? Or if he asks for an egg, will give him a scorpion? If you then, though you are evil, know how to give good gifts to your children, how much more will your Father in heaven give the Holy Spirit to those who ask him!* (vs.10-13)

There are so many fear-of-receiving issues addressed in this passage. The first fear addressed is being afraid that you might not receive. God clearly answers this with the simple phrase, "Everyone who asks receives."

The second fear God addresses is the fear that one could receive something evil from the devil when asking the Father for the Holy Spirit. God uses the common metaphors of the snake and the scorpion to represent the devil. He basically says that if you ask for something good from your Father in Heaven, He will not give you something from the evil one. You can be confident that when you ask for something good, God will protect that transaction. God is a certified secure site for heavenly transactions.

Finally, God addresses the fear that you have not been good enough to receive or that you don't deserve this blessing. God's gifts to us are based upon His goodness, not ours. God is a good Father who knows how to give good things to His children.

If you have never asked God for the gift of prophecy, then do so right now. Ask with confidence knowing that you will receive a good thing from a good

Father. Begin to receive His gift to you by faith. You are receiving God's grace to operate in a certain aspect of God's divine character, power, and nature. Be assured in your heart that something very real and powerful is happening regardless of what you do or do not feel.

### Act upon the gift and grace you have received.

*Do not neglect your gift, which was given you through a prophetic message when the body of elders laid their hands on you* (1 Timothy 4:14).

*Fan into flame the gift...*(2 Timothy 1:6).

Many people wait for some irresistible urge to use their spiritual gifts. God is not looking for robotic followers who have no choice but to obey the commands given. God has always been looking for family, friends, and partners. The supernatural is always God's "super" and your "natural."

## About This Book

The Scripture passages above tell us that it is our responsibility not to neglect our gifts, but rather, to fan them into flame—to stir ourselves to action.

That is what this book is all about.

In the following twelve chapters you will discover many ways to "fan into flame" the gift of God that is within you.

Prophecy should never be a form or formula. The prophetic is meant to be a divine dialogue with the Holy Spirit.

Each of the activations in this book is designed to be a trigger for greater conversation with God. Recall the young boy, Samuel. God was already speaking to him; he just had not yet recognized the ways that God was speaking.[4] The voice of God sounded too natural to him.

Likewise, God is already giving you prophetic words and insights. It might be that you just have not yet come to know the ways that God is speaking prophetically to you. For this reason, the activations are also crafted to help you recognize the many ways God might speak to you prophetically.

Each chapter gives you one clear objective, followed by a study of the biblical basis behind that specific approach to the prophetic. So that you can see how each prophetic principle can be applied in everyday life, I have included in each chapter examples and testimonies from my personal experience and journey . The examples are meant to help you see what this prophetic exercise might look like practically.

There are activations recommended in each chapter, originally designed for group interaction, but we have also adapted them for individuals. In addition, the Appendix of Prophetic Activations includes many more exercises and is organized numerically and alphabetically.

Chapters conclude with discussion and reflection questions crafted to further your understanding of the biblical concepts, along with practical applications for each of the prophetic activations. If you plan on working through *Basic Training for Prophetic Activations* by yourself, I encourage you to invite a few close friends to join you for the activation and discussion portions.

## Prophetic Protocol for Activations

As we prepare to activate the prophetic grace and gifts upon our lives, we will need to lay down some ground rules—or prophetic protocol—for how we will deliver a word. Here are a few guidelines to begin with. You can also adapt other guidelines as you discover what is appropriate within your own culture or spiritual environment.

---

4    1 Samuel 3.

## Be Positive

New Testament prophecy primarily centers around the ministry of encouragement, comfort, and building up another person.[5]

My friend Kris Vallotton, an internationally recognized prophetic trainer, says:

*"Look for the treasure, not the trash."*

Anyone can see negative activity in another person, but it often takes true prophetic grace to see the positive. Kris also teaches that if you don't know whether a word is encouraging or not, then try it out on yourself first and see how you would like it if someone were speaking that word over you.

## Be Brief

A prophetic word does not have to be long to be powerful. In most cases, a single word or phrase is what will really stick in a person's spirit. Deliver the word as clearly and concisely as you can. You do not have to explain the whole picture you see, or the process you went through in receiving the word—just deliver it.

Sometimes people feel more powerful or more prophetic when they are able to speak many words. Giving a long prophetic word does not make you spiritually deep. Jesus was the master of speaking short phrases that were absolutely transformational. In many of our activation exercises, you will only have from one to five minutes to receive and deliver the prophetic word.

So be prepared to be brief and try not to teach the prophetic word—just give it.

---

5  1 Corinthians 14:3.

## Be Kind

I love the words of Galatians 5:6:

*The only thing that counts is faith expressing itself through love.*

First Corinthians chapter 13 really drives home this point: if you have amazing gifts and accuracy but don't have love, it means nothing. Love and kindness can be expressed in a gentle, friendly vocal tone while looking someone kindly in the eyes as you deliver the word with a smiling, bright, and encouraging countenance.

Many people are afraid of prophetic ministry—it feels foreign or spooky. Don't add to their fears with a scrunched-up face, a fiery tone, or harsh, foreboding words. Follow the way of love as you pursue the gift of prophecy.[6]

Kindness also refers to content. There are healthier contexts for delivering correction or direction than through a prophetic word. Correction is better shared in the context of a relational conversation. I will usually only bring correction to someone into whose life I have already made significant deposits. I don't want to withdraw more than I have put in and become relationally overdrawn.

Directional words should also be approached with a certain amount of caution and honor. The receiver of a prophetic word can often fail to judge, process, interpret, or apply the word with the same context and intent it was delivered. For this reason, as a general rule, we do not prophesy about dates, mates, babies, or major life changes. Not because we don't receive this information from time to time, but because it is not always loving, honoring, and wise to deliver it in a prophetic context.

---

6  1 Corinthians 14:1.

## Be Humble

When activating your prophetic grace, there will be times that you miss it or misinterpret what you are seeing. Missing it does not make you a false prophet. A false prophet is not someone with a wrong word, but rather, it is a person with a false motive or attitude. Balaam had the right words but the wrong motive and was called a false prophet.[7]

If you miss it, "clean up your mess." Apologize. Make things right any way that you can, and move on.

Be teachable. Don't defend yourself or insist that you are right. If you are right in something you delivered, it will often be proven in time.

Be humble. You can seldom go wrong by staying low since the yoke and partnership with Jesus is humility and gentleness.[8]

## Be Bold

Take chances. Most people miss supernatural opportunities because what comes to them seems too natural or too simple to be special. Don't wait to be overpowered by God. Know that He is looking for friends, partners, and lovers who are about the Father's business.

Many prophetic impressions come as what I call "drive-bys." It could be as simple as a thought-picture or impression that quickly passes through your mind and spirit. It takes boldness and confidence to speak out those whispers of the Spirit.

The intent of this book is to train you on how to hear from God and activate what you are hearing, seeing, thinking, and perceiving in the form of prophetic words. This will never happen, however, if you allow fear, shyness, and timidity to rule. Be respectfully and reverently cautious but courageously bold.

---

7   See Numbers 22-24, 2 Peter 2:1, Jude 11.
8   Matthew 11:20.

This is a time for learning and maturing. The environment for learning needs to be a safe place of experimentation and a place of mutual good will for exploring, discovering, and mastering the mysteries of the invisible Kingdom.

With these things in mind, we are now ready to begin—or advance—your prophetic journey. Prayerfully partner with the Holy Spirit and Christian friends to step out in your prophetic grace. Grab your Bible, your journal, and a friend, and get ready for the adventure of a lifetime.

God links a person's name to
an element of their prophetic
destiny.

# WHAT'S IN A NAME?

## CHAPTER ONE

*Objective: Prophesy using a name as a prophetic trigger.*

Abraham is an extremely important character in biblical history and our Christian heritage. He is called "the father of the faith." Hearing his name so often, we sometimes forget that his birth name was actually Abram. God changed his name as a prophetic statement when Abram was ninety-nine years old. The biblical account occurs in Genesis:

> *As for me, this is my covenant with you: You will be the father of many nations. No longer will you be called Abram; your name will be Abraham, for I have made you a father of many nations (17:4-5).*

Abram means "exalted father." Abraham means "father of many." God used the meaning of Abram's given name to prophesy concerning his future destiny. He not only endorsed its meaning, but actually upgraded it to a whole different level. Then God made additional prophetic promises based upon on his given name and the new upgrade.

> I will make you very fruitful; I will make nations of you, and kings will come from you. I will establish my covenant as an everlasting covenant between me and you and your descendants after you... The whole land of Canaan, where you are now an alien, I will give as an everlasting possession to you and your descendants after you; and I will be their God (vs. 6-8).

God did the same thing for Abraham's wife, Sarai.[9]

Names are important to God. I do not believe anyone is named by accident. All throughout Scripture, God links a person's name to an element of their prophetic destiny.

This is true in the New Testament as well as the Old. Jesus prophesied over Simon Peter in much the same way that God did over Abraham.

> Jesus replied, "Blessed are you, Simon son of Jonah, for this was not revealed to you by man, but by my Father in heaven. And I tell you that you are Peter, and on this rock I will build my church, and the gates of Hades will not overcome it. I will give you the keys of the kingdom of heaven; whatever you bind on earth will be bound in heaven, and whatever you loose on earth will be loosed in heaven" (Matthew 16:17-19).

Like the account of Abraham, Jesus is prophesying over Simon through the meaning of his name. Simon's name means "a small rock or pebble," but the name, Peter, speaks of a large or solid rock. Here we see that names in both the Old and New Testament are a valid launching pad for giving accurate and encouraging prophetic words.

---

9 Genesis 17:15-16.

There are many ways to prophesy using a name as a prophetic trigger.

## Meanings of Names

I love to memorize the meaning of people's names because it can so often serve as a trigger to start the flow of a prophetic word. The meanings of names are a powerful launch pad for prophecy. If I do not know the meaning of someone's name, I will often ask the person if they know what it means. You can also Google™ the meaning of a name on a mobile device or computer. This form of prophetic encouragement works great with people wearing name tags, and it is always a great conversation starter.

Another great thing about prophesying using names is that it is very affirming to show interest in another person's name.

### Marah

Marah helped serve some of the speakers at a conference I was attending. Her jet black hair hung to her chin in a short crop that often concealed her eyes. It did not take great prophetic insight to interpret her slumping posture and unkempt appearance; Marah had identity issues.

Making friendly eye contact with her, I greeted Marah and asked her if she knew what her name meant.

Marah glanced down at the carpet and replied, "Yes, it means bitter."

I caught her eyes again and said, "Marah, you're not the bitter waters. You are the place where bitter waters become sweet."[10]

Her countenance dawned with a bit of hope as I continued, "I

---

10 Exodus 15:22-25.

believe God has given you a ministry of reconciliation. You have the ability to help people who are bitter of heart or in bitter circumstances to recognize the presence of the Branch, Jesus. You are meant to bring sweetness and life. That is what your name means."

Marah's eyes spilled over with tears. "I have never liked my name. I've even thought about legally changing it."

"But not now..." I interjected.

She smiled widely and shook her head, "Not now," she agreed.

## Famous Characters

Sometimes you will hear or see a person's first or last name and immediately think of a famous biblical character or historical figure. Most often this impression is not something insignificant, but rather, a flash of prophetic insight. As we dialogue with Holy Spirit about the impression, we receive additional information about the similarities between the famous person and the one bearing the name.

### Michael

Michael waited patiently in line to receive prophetic ministry. Though the young, slightly husky twenty-something lacked the towering height of a basketball player, I immediately had a flash of the famous ball-handler, Michael Jordan. I quickly asked for direction from Holy Spirit and heard the phrase "game-changer." I remembered the basketball star's uncanny ability to take charge of a game and change its course.

With a confirming sense that I was on the right track I started in, "Michael, I feel like you are a game-changer. You are one who is able to take responsibility for atmospheres and situations and then alter the course and outcome..." Continuing along these lines

I encouraged Michael in what turned out to be a very confirming word in his life.

## Sounds Similar

Though I am not a Greek or Hebrew scholar, I am told that some prophetic declarations in Scripture may be based upon a subtle play on words. Every prophetic impression should be in cooperation and leading of the Holy Spirit, but often these will come and go at the speed of light. You must grab hold of your faith and step out with these flash impressions. If someone introduced themselves as Mikey, but you heard or read their name as "my key," this may be a launch pad for a prophetic word. Check in with Holy Spirit for confirmation, then begin to speak about whatever "key" you feel the Lord has given them.

### Stan

Stan's grip as we shook hands carried the force of a vice. His weathered hands and face spoke of years of dues he had paid working the field in harsh conditions.

When I heard his name, I heard the word "stand," along with the Scripture from Ephesians, "after you have done everything to stand...stand firm then..."[11] I perceived by the Spirit that Stan was on the edge of a crucial decision and was tempted to give in to some external pressure, but God was giving him the strength to stand his ground. I saw a flash vision of the Lord pouring steel and concrete into his back and midsection to make his resolve strong and his foundation sure.

Stan wrote later to inform me that he was indeed in the midst of a business deal where all the voices around him were trying to get him to lower his price. He had been claiming the exact Scripture I

---

11 Ephesians 6:13b, 14a.

quoted over him. He stood his ground in a two-hundred thousand dollar business deal and won the account.

Learning to pay close attention to the names of people we meet will give us clues about prophetic encouragement God wants to give them, often at a strategic time in their lives.

# Recommended Prophetic Activations

## 1  Prophetic Name Game

*This is an activation using the name of a person to get prophetic clues.*

1. If you are in a group, divide into smaller groups of two or three. Prophesy over each other using one of the three name methods[12] as a trigger for prophetic encouragement.

   A. Meaning of names

   B. Famous characters

   C. Sounds similar

2. For individual activation, craft a prophetic encouragement based upon the name of a friend. Then send it to him or her via email or cell phone text message.

## 2  Prophetic Name Badges  I

*Make it a habit to practice prophecy that is triggered by names wherever people wear name tags. You can also ask the Lord about those you deal with in the business world and marketplace on a regular basis. In this way, you can regularly arm and prepare yourself for prophetic activation.*

1. If you're in a group that can travel, go on a field trip to places

---

12    Refer to Chapter One "What's in a Name" for a review of these methods.

where people wear name tags: markets, banks, restaurants, etc.

2. Look for people who are not busy with customers or their work. Prophesy over that person with a short word of encouragement related to their name.

3. If you are reading through this book by yourself, think of people who regularly wait on you at the bank, the grocery store checkout, a favorite restaurant waiter. Ask the Lord for prophetic insights that relate to their names. Print out the results you get and be prepared to share it the next time you see these persons.

## 3 Favorite Bible Character

*Ask the members of your group to choose a favorite Bible character—the one they most admire in character and actions.*

1. Have each one in the group go person-to-person, introducing themselves by the name of their favorite Bible character.

2. Each person will prophesy over the other from a quality that relates to that specific Bible character.

3. If you are studying this book by yourself, ask God for prophetic insights on why you relate to this Bible character. Write the results as a prophetic word in your journal.

## 4 Assigned Identities

*If God renamed you, what new name would He give you?*

1. In a group setting, pair up and have each group member assign a

new identity to his partner by changing his name.

2. Prophesy over your partner about why you would give that particular name and describe its prophetic significance.

3. If you are by yourself, ask the Lord for a new name, or choose one, and then research the meaning. Write all of your research and revelation down in the form of a prophetic word for yourself.

# 5  Most Common Name

*This activation helps prepare you to receive revelation surrounding the most common names. Wikipedia, the free online encyclopedia, lists the most popular given names for every country of the world. In the United States, the top boys' names in 2011 were: Jacob, Mason, William, Jayden, Noah, Michael, Ethan, Alexander, Aiden, Daniel. The most common girls' names were: Sophia, Isabella, Emma, Olivia, Ava, Emily, Abigail, Madison, Mia, Chloe.*[13]

*Feel free to use a different list of common names related to your geographic region.*

1. Write each one of these popular names on a separate 3x5 index card with a dark marker pen.

2. Place the cards in a hat and have volunteers draw a card out of the hat. The person reads the selected name and then has 30 seconds to deliver a prophetic word related to that name.

3. If you are processing this book by yourself, use the index cards

---

13   www.ssa.gov/oact/babynames/

like flash cards, giving different prophetic words related to each name.

# 6 Surname Sounds-Like

*Surname is another term for your last name or family name. In this activation group members will use the sounds-like exercise to prophesy over surnames.*

*For example, my last name is McCollam. It sounds like "call 'em." So, someone might prophesy over me about calling in leaders or calling in the lost.*

*In another example, you are talking to a person who has Smith as a surname. You could prophesy about him being a craftsman with words, or with details, or being sharpened by the Lord.*

1. Have several volunteers stand before your group and share their last names one at a time.

2. Allow volunteers who are seated to give short prophetic encouragements using this sounds-like exercise.

3. After a few words have been given, move on to the next volunteer. Continue on until the group has practiced on three to five volunteers.

4. If you are processing by yourself, use the last names of your three closest friends. Write out prophetic encouragement based on this sounds-like exercise for each of these friends. Be prepared to share it with them at an appropriate time.

## 7 Blind Phone Book Find

*If this is for a group, collect as many local phone books as you can find. Get in small groups of three to five and provide a phone book for each group.*

1.  Have one group member fan through the phone book pages while the member to the right has his eyes closed.

2.  The member with his eyes closed places a finger on a random name in the phone book. Read the name aloud and give a prophetic word for that person using one of the name methods.

3.  Then pass the phone book to the left and continue until everyone in the group has had at least one turn.

4.  While doing this exercise, you may feel strongly about the prophetic word you have given. If so, call the person and actually deliver this word of encouragement to them. You could say something like, "You don't know me, but I saw your name in the phone book and feel like God wants to share something with you. Would you like to hear it?" If they decline then let them go; if they say "yes," then share the word the Lord leads you to say. Note: Because this is a stranger you are talking to, do not give out any personal information or contact details over the phone. If they ask for contact information, give your local church name, phone number, address, etc.

5.  You can perform the same activation on your own. Put the phone book in front of you. Close your eyes and flip quickly through the pages. Without looking, plop your finger down on a name and practice prophesying over the name that is closest to where your finger points.

# Discussion and Reflection Questions

1. Can you think of other scriptural examples of a prophetic word that was based upon a name? What are they? Why do you think God changed people's names? (Examples: Abram to Abraham, Jacob to Israel, and Simon to Peter, etc.)

_____

_____

2. Have you used the name trigger to prophesy prior to reading this chapter? How did you use it and what was the result?

_____

_____

3. Which of the three name trigger methods is most comfortable for you and why?

_____

_____

4. What are some ways and locations where you could use this method to bring prophetic words and encouragement into your current life routine?

_____

_____

# Notes

God can use both internal
and external vision to inspire a
genuine prophetic word.

# WHAT DO YOU SEE?

## CHAPTER TWO

*Objective: Utilize physical objects as catalysts for prophetic encouragement and insight.*

God trained Old Testament prophets by asking the question, "What do you see?"

*The word of the LORD came to me: "What do you see, Jeremiah?"*

*"I see the branch of an almond tree," I replied.*

*The LORD said to me, "You have seen correctly, for I am watching to see that my word is fulfilled."*

*The word of the LORD came to me again: "What do you see?"*

*"I see a boiling pot, tilting away from the north," I answered* (Jeremiah 1:11-13).

In this passage, we do not know if Jeremiah's visions were internal or external; that is, we do not know if the prophet was seeing these things with his natural eyes or in a spiritual vision. Later, however, we know that God used natural vision to stimulate a prophetic declaration.

*This is the word that came to Jeremiah from the LORD: "Go down to the potter's house, and there I will give you my message"* (Jeremiah 18:1).

As Jeremiah watched the potter work with the clay, he received inspiration for a prophetic word from the Lord. It is evident from Scripture that God can use both internal and external vision to inspire a genuine prophetic word or declaration.

God used this method of training prophets with external images as the catalyst for prophetic words for Jeremiah, Amos, and Zechariah.[14]

# Prophesying Using External Objects

Since we can see the validity of using external objects as a catalyst for prophetic information, let's explore some of the ways that this type of inspiration begins.

## Clothing and Accessories

Though we should never judge by appearances, we all understand that clothing and accessories can be an outward expression of inward realities. It's when an outward object is quickened to your attention that it can be used as a

---

14  See Amos 7:8, 8:2, and Zechariah 4:2, 5:2.

launch pad for a prophetic word. This quickening often starts as a heightened attention to a specific detail—being really drawn to the color of a shirt, for instance, or a necklace, or shoes.

After a realization of heightened awareness, we check with Holy Spirit for confirmation. Confirmation can reveal itself in many different forms, from an inward peace, to a continued pressure, or a compulsion to speak. Heightened attention or focus to an external detail can come with a flood of additional information and ideas, or with a single, focused thought. A lack of confirmation would be any negative sensation about moving forward, a sudden dissipation or evaporation of the heightened awareness, or a flood of information in a contrary direction.

The more you take risks to speak out prophetic encouragement the more you will learn to recognize how Holy Spirit leads you.

## The Watch

Pastor Craig and I sat in the overstuffed chairs of his informal living room near a crackling fire. Our after-dinner discussion turned towards how Holy Spirit leads us in prophetic encouragement, and Craig then mentioned how he uses jewelry as a trigger. Intrigued by that idea, I asked him to explain the concept further.

"It's like your wrist watch," he said. "I'm suddenly drawn to your watch."

I looked down at my Blue Angel Skyhawk watch that was a recent gift from a friend.

Craig continued, "That watch has every time zone of the world on it. I see the Lord taking you into many nations and giving you great impact and influence around the world."

When Craig spoke these words, I actually didn't know much about that watch, and I had not yet traveled very often outside of the United States.

Since this prophetic word, however, I have flown more than 100,000 miles each year to countries on five continents. The majority of my ministry now takes place outside the United States.

Pastor Craig's words, sparked by my wristwatch, had a lasting impact on my life. Since that encounter, I have often used clothing, jewelry, and shoes as a launch pad for accurate and encouraging prophetic words.

## Surrounding Objects

As I mentioned earlier in this chapter, God used natural items in everyday surroundings as inspiration for messages to people. The two questions God would often ask are "What do you see?" and "What does it mean?"

These questions are still powerful today in perceiving what God is speaking to the hearts and lives of people. Look at your surroundings and see where your attention lands. Ask God if He is speaking something through your inward drawing to that specific focal point.

As I write this chapter, my attention is drawn to the large table in our dining room. The table's robust, routed legs and natural planked surface was chosen to create a comfortable and welcoming environment for hospitality. In this moment I feel like God is speaking to you, the reader, and saying that He has prepared a bountiful prophetic table for you. The enemy wants you to feel like you just have scraps or crumbs to offer in this regard, but God is welcoming you to a huge prophetic feast where you can taste and see that He is good. You have something prophetic and encouraging for everyone who comes hungry and sincere. Even in the presence of your enemies, there will be a table of prophetic insights and blessings pouring from your mouth.

So do not be afraid to let God speak through all that surrounds you. He is always with you, and He is always speaking.

## Intentional Objects

God spoke to the prophet Ezekiel and told him to bring specific objects with him that were related to what God wanted to communicate to His people.

*Take a clay tablet...take an iron pan...take wheat and barley, beans and lentils, millet and spelt; put them in a storage jar...take a sharp sword...take a set of scales*[15]*...*

Each of these physical elements had been intentionally introduced into the environment as part of what God desired to speak.

### Mr. Potato Head

Tammy stands just over five feet tall with beautiful blonde hair and penetrating eyes. She leads our intercessory prayer team at my home church and has been a close family friend and accurate prophetic voice for many years.

One chilly winter Sunday morning at our church service, Tammy approached me with something concealed in her closed hand.

"Dano," Tammy said, "the Lord shared with me how you have been wrestling with your personal identity." The truthfulness and insight of those words struck me like an arrow to the heart.

"God sent me with something to give you that is going to help you with your identity."

Excitement and anticipation sprang up in my heart with the internal pressure of an artesian well. Tammy held out her clenched hand...*What would this symbol of my new identity be?* I

---

15    Ezekiel 4:1, 3, 9; 5:1.

wondered. Now I could finally rest from my desperate search for some assignment to hang my sense of personal worth upon!

I leaned closer to see what awesome treasure Tammy held in her hand. Slowly she opened up her palm to reveal…a Mr. Potato Head Happy Meal toy? Wow…

I have to say that my heart sank a bit. I might have even felt a little insulted at first.

Tammy's laugh depressurized the moment. "You are not to get your identity in this season from what you do," Tammy said to me. "God will have many different assignments and faces for you. You are to simply rejoice in Him and be His son. Whatever face or assignment He puts on you is up to Him. Just relax and rejoice in the Lord."

Though it was not exactly what I hoped to hear in that moment, this was a great and enduring word in my life that helped me learn the secret of rejoicing in sonship over function.

From this word, I also learned to multitask. However, whenever, and whatever God assigned me to do, I did it with joy and thanksgiving. From that point on I began to live in a joyful, fruitful season initiated by a faithful servant and a Mr. Potato Head figure.

# Recommended Prophetic Activations

## 1 Appearance Triggers

*For this exercise remember not to judge by appearances, but rather, allow the Lord to draw your attention to a specific detail that triggers a word of prophetic encouragement. Consider that colors, shapes, letters, and numbers can all be a part of triggering the prophetic flow.*

1. Get with a friend or a small group and practice prophetic encouragement triggered by an item of clothing, jewelry, shoes, words that appear on clothing, or even tattoos.

2. If you are processing this book by yourself, flip through magazines looking for external triggers for the prophetic through what people are wearing.

## 2 Environmental Triggers

*This activation is a good opportunity to become more aware of our external environment, recognizing that God will use these as clues to give a prophetic encouraging word for someone.*

1. Pair up with a friend or gather a small group.
2. Look around the room and observe your surroundings for something that might immediately attract your attention. Perhaps it is the "exit" sign or a big comfy chair, or maybe you are drawn to a bookshelf, a podium, chalkboard, or an eraser.
3. Take turns in your small group sharing about the item that triggered your attention and what you felt the Lord was speaking through that item.

4. Those activating this book by themselves can journal the things that God is speaking to them through their external environment.

## 3 Table of Triggers

*For a small to medium-sized group, bring five or six various and seemingly "random" items to trigger prophetic encouragements. Place all items on a table in front of the group.*

1. Have one volunteer from the group choose an item off of the table.

2. Have two or three other volunteers from the group share an encouraging prophetic word with the person who chose the item, using that item as a trigger from which to prophesy.

3. After the prophetic words about that person from the specific item have been shared, select a new volunteer. The new volunteer may choose any item on the table, including the one that was just recently selected.

Get three new volunteers to give a prophetic word triggered from that item.

## 4 Postcard Prophecy

*Have the people in your group bring six to ten postcards or small art prints of various subjects. This exercise will activate prophetic words from these visual clues.*

1. Select a volunteer from the group to choose the photo they are most drawn to.

2. Ask the group to share prophetic encouragements for that volunteer based on the selected photo.

3. Follow this pattern a more few times with different volunteers, each one selecting a card and the rest of the group giving prophetic feedback.

4. Then ask each person in the group to choose one of the cards and journal a personal prophetic word based on the photo they have chosen.

5. Those activating by themselves can choose a piece of artwork in their home, a picture from a magazine, or an advertisement in the mail and journal what the Lord is speaking through that picture.

## 5 Prophetic Gift Exchange

*This activation trains you to see the prophetic meaning behind a gift.*

1. Print the names of your group members on cards or small slips of paper.

2. Pass out the name cards to each member of the group.

3. Have your group members return the following week with an item from home or something inexpensive purchased from the store that prophetically represents something they feel the Lord is speaking into the life of the person whose name they received.

4. Gather your group in a circle and have them present their gifts one-by-one along with what the Lord is saying through that gift.

## 6 White Elephant Prophetic Gift Exchange

*Plan a "white elephant" prophetic gift exchange with some friends or family members.*

1. Each person participating buys or brings a small gift from home with a prophetic word they received written down and attached to it.

2. Wrap the gifts so that no one knows what they are.

3. Each person in attendance chooses a gift from the table, opens it and reads out loud the prophetic encouragement accompanying the gift.

## 7 Internal Triggers

*In this activation divide the group into pairs. Instead of activating with external objects alone, you will use your inner eyesight or sanctified imagination. Remember, each word should be according to our prophetic protocol—encouraging, strengthening, or comforting.*

1. Close your eyes for just a moment and ask the Lord for a picture for the other person. Do you see a still picture, a movie, a flash of color?

2. Share what you see for the other person and what you think it means.

## Discussion and Reflection Questions

1. Have you previously had external objects or someone's appearance quickened to you but not known that it was God focusing your attention to these details? Now that you know that a quickening to external details is one of the ways that God can speak, how might you use this method of prophetic encouragement in your everyday life?

   _____

   _____

2. Read Psalm 19 and Romans 1:19-20. How might these Scriptures relate to God's desire to speak through our external surroundings?

   _____

   _____

3. Read the following Scriptures: Isaiah 11:3, 1 Samuel 16:7, and John 7:24.

   A. What do you feel is the difference between judging by appearances and being quickened to external details?

   _____

   _____

   B. What safe guards should we put in place to keep us from merely judging by appearances?

_____

_____

C. When it comes to the prophetic, would you say that you are more often triggered by an external image or an internal vision?

_____

_____

D. Have you ever been given a gift that had a prophetic significance to you? What was the gift and how did it speak to you?

_____

_____

# Notes

Written words
have shaped the mindsets of
generations and turned the course
of nations.

# PROPHECY AND WRITTEN WORDS

## CHAPTER THREE

*Objective: Activate the power of the written word in prophecy.*

n 1839, English author Edward Bulwer-Lytton wrote the famous words, "The pen is mightier than the sword." Words written down have truly shaped the mindsets of generations and turned the course of nations. Among all written words, none compares with the Bible.

> *For the word of God is living and active. Sharper than any double-edged sword, it penetrates even to dividing soul and spirit, joints and marrow; it judges the thoughts and attitudes of the heart* (Hebrews 4:12).

God's Word is alive. It radically alters those who hear and choose to do it. The Word itself has the power to penetrate into the deepest part of the human heart. It is no wonder it is also a powerful tool for prophetic ministry. Perhaps that is why Jesus quoted from Old Testament Scriptures 78 times in His public ministry. The preaching of Jesus is so laced with prophecy that it is difficult, and probably not necessary, to separate the two. It suffices to say that the earthly ministry of Jesus Christ validates the practice of quoting Scripture as a means of prophetic encouragement.

Scripture also cites the use of non-biblical or extra-biblical sources for ministry. When Nathan the Prophet was confronting King David, he used a prophetic story, or parable, to prepare the king's heart to receive the word from the Lord.[16] Likewise, Paul quoted a modern poet of the day when ministering to the group at Mars Hill.[17]

These examples give us context for using creative writing in all its forms to convey a prophetic word.

# Prophesying Using Written Words

## Prophecy Triggered from Scripture Passages

Memorizing Scripture is a great way to prepare yourself for prophetic ministry. From what you have memorized, God can quicken your heart to share a specific word with an individual. You can also read devotionally each day, not only to get a fresh word for your own life, but also to equip yourself to minister to others.

### A Powerful Prophetic Word

My lovely wife, Regina, and I received our first prophetic word nearly thirty years ago in a lively revival church in the Greater

---

16   2 Samuel 12.
17   Acts 17:28.

Cincinnati area. The guest speaker that night spoke with a smooth, southern drawl, and wore a crisp suit and power tie. He always started his prophetic words by calling out someone's name and then saying, "I have a word from the Lord for you and it is found in the book of..." Then the classy preacher would progress quoting a significant scriptural passage or promise. After sharing the Scripture, the speaker would begin to elaborate on what God was saying prophetically.

Thirty years later, I can truly say, that every word of that first prophecy given to us by this seasoned preacher came true and held a powerful place in our lives.

Scripture is a great launching pad for powerful prophetic ministry.

## Prophecy through Creative Writing

Sharing something that you have written requires a lot of vulnerability. Because of this, when people have the opportunity to read something in your presence which you have written, they are usually more open, tender, and caring in how they respond.

This vulnerability of the creator and the reader creates a great opening for giving and receiving prophetic ministry.

### A Prophetic Song

Among the towering redwoods of the North Coast of California, I taught at a YWAM (Youth With A Mission) base where the buildings were all carved from the local wood giving it the shire-like appearance of a J. R. Tolkien novel. With a crisp ocean fog rolling across the treetops, we settled near a crackling fire to share stories about our prophetic experiences.

One of those stories came from a flannel-clad young man who had composed a story-song about a single mother's struggle with her terminally ill child. Toward the end of the song the young mother cried out to God for help.

The young man shared how one day he was eating at a local café in the small coastal village nearby. As he ate, he struck up a conversation with a young waitress whose face mirrored the weariness of her soul. Much to his surprise, the waitress turned out to be living in the exact situation of the song he had written. Before she could elaborate on her personal details, the young man pulled the lyrics out of his folder and let her read the story in song. Though she was not a follower of Christ at the time, when she got to the end of the story, tears were streaming down her face and she began to call out to God.

Little did he know that this bit of creative writing was actually a prophetic word that would change someone's life.

## Prophecy through Written Communication

With social networks, email, cell phone texting, and the like, we are constantly connecting with people through written communication. Because people in most cultures today are comfortable with this form of communication, it can make a great bridge for delivering a prophetic word. It is so affirming when someone writes to you saying something like, "I was praying for you today, and I feel like the Lord spoke something to my heart for you."

### New Wineskin

I received an email from a friend containing this word:

I saw you at a fork in the road. One road has an old wineskin attached to it and the other a new one. I saw a natural draw to the old wine skin. There's enlargement, an inheritance available for you in this season through this new wineskin. I saw you walking in a holding pattern. Today is the day of decision.

I see the word "father" attached to the new wineskin as well with sources of life sprouting simultaneously. It is not to be confusing to you; it is about fathering.

Your fruit in this season is going to begin to self-duplicate and self-represent. You aren't even going to be present and yet, you'll be reaping. Wow! So strong.

I see a repositioning of how you think geographically. It is going to be a whole new strategy, maybe with similar tools, but a new end-goal. It's deeper and more mature now.

I knew exactly what this word was talking about even though the friend who wrote it had no knowledge of my current circumstance and lived thousands of miles away.

These types of written prophetic words can be so encouraging. It is so great to know that you have friends who can hear from God.

We want to continue to enlarge our ability to prophetically communicate in creative ways.

# Recommended Prophetic Activations

## 1 Psalm 23 Prophecy

*This is a great practice for every believer to use during devotional times, not only to feed yourself through the Word and prayer, but also to "pack a lunch" for others. As you are reading, write down Scriptures that stir your heart as they may be for someone else you meet or talk with during the day. Look for opportunities to share the Scriptures you have written down, memorized, or meditated upon. Always have a word like this on your heart, and you will greatly increase the number of divine appointments in your daily life.*

*For this exercise, have each person read Psalm 23.*

1. Divide the group into pairs.

2. Each person in the pair will look over Psalm 23 and choose one verse or phrase that stands out to him in that moment. The chosen verses will become the foundation for prophetic encouragements given to each other. For instance, you might start with the verse, "He anoints my head with oil," and then say, "I see the Lord giving you a fresh anointing; it may also involve promotion in a specific area." Here's another example: "He makes me lie down in green pastures and leads me beside the still waters." You could then encourage the person with something like, "I see a season of rest and refreshing for you. God is calming the waters surrounding you and leading you into rest and stillness. In that place you will find fresh revelation and new purpose to your doing."

3. Remember, in this exercise, use only one line of the Psalm as a prophetic trigger to speak over your partner.

4. For individual activation, choose the scriptural phrase that really stands out to you and ask the Lord what He is saying to you from that verse. In a journal, write down what Lord is speaking to you.

## 2  Phone-a-Friend Prophecy

*Make this exercise a regular practice of sending prophetic words and encouragement to friends and family through email, social networks, and phone text messages.*

1. Choose someone from your cell phone contacts, social network or email contacts list to prophesy over.

2. Compose a prophetic message in the form of a cell phone text or email message. Because this form of communication is characteristically short, condense your prophetic words down to as few lines as possible. You can start the message with something like, "I was thinking of you today and felt like I heard..."

3. Prayerfully send the message.

## 3  Secret Friend Prophetic Letter

*Set up this activation by explaining that each person will write out a prophetic word. They do not know for whom they are writing, but God knows. Therefore, they can trust that the word will be led of the Spirit. In actuality, the prophetic word is being written for themselves.*

*This activation reveals that not only can we hear from God to prophesy over others, but God can also speak to us significantly and prophetically about our own identity, destiny and current situations.*

1. Give everyone about ten minutes to pray and write out the mystery word.

2. After the time is up, announce to everyone that the mystery word they received is actually for themselves personally!

3. This is a great exercise to activate on your own as often as possible. Allow God to encourage you personally in this way, and you will have something significant to share with someone He sends into your life today.

## 4 Creative Prophetic Writing

*The idea of this exercise is to prepare a prophetic word that is embedded in some form of creative writing. This type of written prophecy works great to share with pre-Christians or those who might not otherwise be open to prophetic ministry.*

1. Prepare a short story, a poem, a song, or devotional thought in written form.

2. This activation is a "carry-out" exercise. People will carry the word with them to work, school, or their neighborhood, watching for opportunities to share it with the right person.

3. Usually the person the creative prophetic writing piece was intended for is someone you already know. If this is the case, you can simply open a conversation with that person by saying, "I wrote a little something (i.e., story, poem, song, inspirational thought) the other day and wondered if you would like to read it?" If it seems appropriate, you can follow up by saying, "I felt like God had me write that specifically for you."

Many times this will make a real connection with the person and open up the opportunity for a deeper conversation on spiritual matters.

# 5 Favorite Line Prophecy

*Just like we use Scripture and our own creative writing as a trigger for prophetic ministry, we can also use what others have written. Often, a catalyst for a prophetic word can come from a line of a song, or a line from a book, or the dialogue of a movie.*

*Sometimes, when God is speaking, you will hear a song in your head or see a short clip from a movie run through your imagination. I have learned that God really loves to speak through story and song. God is both timeless and contemporary. He is even up on movies, books, and songs from today's market.*

1. Divide into groups of two or three. Ask the Lord to give you quotes from poems, books, songs, or movies for each other. Confirm this leading in your heart with the Lord, and then share with the other person what you are hearing from God.

2. For individual activation, ask the Lord what He is speaking over you personally. Let Him sing a song over you, or, He may even quote a line from your favorite movie.

# Discussion and Reflection Questions

1. Have you ever read from a morning devotional or a Bible-reading plan and felt like the Scripture assigned to that day was speaking directly to you? Describe your experience. What does this tell you about the prophetic potential of the Scripture? How could you better prepare yourself to use Scripture as a prophetic trigger in daily life?

   _____

   _____

2. Have you ever shared a Scripture passage with someone else in a way that turned out to be prophetic? Share one experience. How could you better prepare yourself for these types of divine appointments?

   _____

   _____

3. Has a book, story, poem, or movie ever inspired you prophetically? Give a short example. Do you have a current personal expression of creative writing—songs, poems, short stories, novels, plays, or devotional? If not, have you ever done this in the past? Have you ever dreamed about doing one of these types of creative expression?

   _____

   _____

4. Have you ever received a text message, email, or viewed a posting on

a social network that spoke to you in a timely prophetic way? Share any experiences you have had in the past using text, instant messages, email, or social network postings for prophetic ministry. If you have never done this before, prepare a plan of action to try this exercise.

_____

_____

5. From your friends and contacts lists, who would you want to share this type of prophetic ministry with?

_____

_____

6. How often will you aim for practicing this type of prophetic ministry?

_____

_____

# Notes

The new man can be trained
in sensitivity to discern
spiritual information through
physical senses.

# TRAINING YOUR SENSES

## CHAPTER FOUR

*Objective: Learn to use your five physical senses as a catalyst for prophetic information.*

Let's consider the valuable role of our senses as we process the world around us through discernment.

> *But solid food is for the mature, who because of practice have their senses trained to discern good and evil* (Hebrews 5:14 NASB).

Some believe that our five senses are merely a gate of information to the natural world. I have found that senses in the natural man tend toward sensuality, but senses in the new man can be trained in sensitivity to discern spiritual information. The contrast between sensuality and sensitivity is highlighted in Ephesians.

*Having lost all sensitivity, they have given themselves over to sensuality so as to indulge in every kind of impurity, with a continual lust for more (4:19).*

Scripture gives us examples of the use of the five senses in the formulation of prophetic words: seeing, hearing, tasting, smelling, and touching. We've already studied in Chapter Two how God used both external and internal sight to train Old Testament prophets.[18]

Sight, or vision, is the ability of the brain and eye to detect electromagnetic waves within the visible range of light. We know it is valid for information discerned through the natural sense of sight to be used in delivering a prophetic message. We see this in how God sent Jeremiah to the potter's house to receive a word from the Lord.

*This is the word that came to Jeremiah from the LORD: "Go down to the potter's house, and there I will give you my message" (Jeremiah 18:1).*

Physical hearing, or audition, is the sound perception sense. God trained the prophet Samuel through hearing the audible voice of the Lord. We have the account in 1 Samuel chapter three.

*Now Samuel did not yet know the LORD: The word of the LORD had not yet been revealed to him. The LORD called Samuel a third time, and Samuel got up and went to Eli and said, "Here I am; you called me." Then Eli realized that the LORD was calling the boy. So Eli told Samuel, "Go and lie down, and if he calls you, say, 'Speak, LORD, for your servant is listening.'" So Samuel went and lay down in his place (vs.7-9).*

We know that God gives prophetic voice through both the physical and

---

18  See Jeremiah 1:11, 1:13, 24:3, Amos 7:8, 8:2, and Zechariah 4:2, 5:2.

internal hearing. The spiritual internal hearing is the main message to the seven churches in the book of Revelation.[19]

> *He who has an ear, let him hear what the Spirit says to the churches...(2:7).*

While seeing and hearing are considered mechanical senses, taste or gustation is one of the two main chemical senses. The prophet Ezekiel was told to eat a scroll to receive the word of the Lord.

> *Then he said to me, "Son of man, eat what is before you, eat this scroll I am giving you and fill your stomach with it." So I ate it, and it tasted as sweet as honey in my mouth. He then said to me: "Son of man, go now to the house of Israel and speak my word to them"* (Ezekiel 3:3-4).

Simon Peter may have been perceiving through the sense of taste when he discerned the heart of Simon the Sorcerer.

> *For I see* [the Greek language would suggest the word "perceive"] *that you are in the gall of bitterness and in the bondage of iniquity* (Acts 8:23 NASB).

Smell, or olfaction, is the other of the two chemical senses. Fragrance is one of the ways that Jesus was described in Old Testament prophecies.

> *His shoots will sprout, and his beauty will be like the olive tree, and his fragrance like the cedars of Lebanon* (Hosea 14:6, NASB).

> *I am the Rose of Sharon, the lily of the valleys* (Song of Songs. 2:1, NASB).

---

19  See also Revelation 2:11, 2:17, 2:29, 3:6, 3:13, 3:22.

Several Old Testament prophets also encountered the Lord through the mechanical sense of touch or tactician. Daniel received several touches from the Lord that resulted in prophetic information.[20] Jeremiah was not only trained by visual senses but also through a touch of the Lord.

> *Then the LORD stretched out His hand and touched my mouth, and the LORD said to me, "Behold I have put My words in your mouth"* (Jeremiah 1:9, NASB).

All of what we call the "natural five senses" was originally designed by God to perceive Him and His Kingdom. As a new creation, we can retrain our senses from mere sensuality to sensitivity to what the Lord is saying.

## How to Prophesy Using Your Senses

Once we determine that our senses are not just a part of the fallen man or evil sinful nature, we can offer the members of our body to Christ for the purposes of righteousness.

> *Do not offer the parts of your body to sin, as instruments of wickedness, but rather offer yourselves to God, as those who have been brought from death to life; and offer the parts of your body to him as instruments of righteousness* (Romans 6:13).

> *Just as you used to offer the parts of your body in slavery to impurity and to ever-increasing wickedness, so now offer them in slavery to righteousness leading to holiness* (6:19).

Let's take a moment to put these Scriptures into practice. Take a little time right now to offer your five senses to the Lord. I know that you have already surrendered yourself wholly to Him through salvation, but now consciously

---

20  See Daniel 8:18. 10:10 and 10:18 as examples.

give your senses to God as instruments of righteous perception.

> Lord, I offer you my eyes that I might see things that trigger prophetic information.
>
> I give you my ears to hear what the Spirit of the Lord is saying.
>
> I give you my nose and tongue to perceive the flavors and fragrances that you want to communicate to me.
>
> Lord, touch me and make me fully sensitive to spiritual information through my senses.
>
> Train me to use these in righteousness. In Jesus' name, amen.

Now that you have offered the members of your body, expect God to communicate to you through each of your five senses.

Just like any other spiritual information we receive for prophecy, we should judge the impression before delivering it. We ask the same questions:

❖ Is it consistent with Scripture?

❖ Is it encouraging?

❖ Does it convey wisdom and peace from God?

Remember that Hebrews 5:14 talks of training your senses through exercise. The word used here for "training" is the Greek word *gymnazo,* which is like our word "gymnasium."

Take your senses "to the gym" and work them out to receive and perceive spiritual information.

How do you do that? Simply consider that a taste, smell, sound, sight, or feeling could be spiritual information.

Have you ever been in worship or prayer and smelled a sweet fragrance like a perfume? That is often a spiritual perception of the Lord's presence with your natural senses. In the same way, a person might give off a spiritual smell or flavor that can be detected by the natural senses but is unexplainable by external causes.

## Chuck

Chuck had four different master's degrees, but with his tattered army fatigues and shaggy hair and beard, he could easily be mistaken for a homeless person. Chuck's passion was street evangelism and his choice of clothing and appearance was part of his "undercover" operation. Chuck not only had his senses exercised for righteousness, but when he prayed for people, they would often have a spiritual perception with their natural senses.

One day in the chilly moors of Northern England, Chuck prayed for a pre-Christian who suddenly could smell the fragrance of his father's aftershave. There was no natural source to the perception since Chuck didn't use aftershave, and his personal fragrance of choice was whatever nature provided. Through the man's perception of smell, Chuck began to prophesy that his Heavenly Father was demonstrating His presence and His nearness in that moment. The man had a life-changing encounter through the simple gate of his senses.

Chuck's story gives a whole new meaning to the passage in Second Corinthians.

*For we are a fragrance of Christ to God among those who are being saved and among those who are perishing; to the one an aroma from death to death, to the other an aroma from life to life...(2:15-16, NASB).*

## Flavors on the Tongue

I did a prophetic training a few years ago in a beautiful coastal city off the tip of South Africa. At this meeting, I was approached by a stately, older man with tears in his eyes.

"I have prayed for years to be able to hear from God," he said. "Often when I pray I get flavors on my tongue, but I never knew it was a spiritual thing."

I nodded as he continued. "Today, I know that all of this time God has been answering my prayer. He was speaking to me through flavors."

That week the man began to prophesy over others using the flavors he would perceive through his natural taste buds. Several people were greatly blessed and encouraged by the words he shared from the trigger of those natural perceptions.

The man who had been a believer most of his life gained great confidence in his ability to minister prophetic encouragement.

Prophetic encouragement could be triggered by something you see in the natural, in your imagination, or in your spirit. You might actually hear an audible sound or suddenly think of a song or a line from a movie that is so strong it is as if you were hearing it with your ears. A flavor or fragrance can also trigger a word of prophecy. You might literally smell and taste or you may have only the perception.

Touch, or tactician, is also one of our five senses. When ministering to someone you may feel a heaviness—or a lightness—on your body. An area of your body may start to burn, tingle, or even experience a form of pain. Prophetic information can also feel like a hand on your shoulder or a kiss on the cheek.

Any of these types of sensations are a unique form of sensitivity to spiritual communication.

# Recommended Prophetic Activations

## 1  What Color Do You See?

*A simple exercise we often use when training children in the prophetic is to ask the question, "What color do you see?"*

1. Divide into pairs.

2. Have each person share what color he sees or perceives on, over, or around the other person.

3. With adults doing this exercise, take the perception further and have them explain why they believe they are seeing that particular color and what it might mean.

4. For those doing these activations on your own, target three leaders in your life with the same question, "What color do you see?"

5. What color do you see on or over your pastor?

6. How about an employer, teacher or adult leader?

7. You can also choose a family member and try to determine what color you see on, over, or around them.

Journal these perceptions and watch to see if God provides an opportunity in the future where you could share these insights in an encouraging way.

## 2  What Flavor Are You?

*This exercise is much like "What Color Do you See?" You may experience a literal taste that comes into your mouth or a perceived taste in your imagination as a spiritual impression.*

1. Divide the group into pairs.

2. Ask for a perception of flavor concerning the other person. Share a prophetic word that is triggered by the perception of flavor.

3. Another way to do this exercise is to ask the Lord, "What flavor is this day?" Dialogue with the Lord for an impression of flavor for this day and why.

4. Journal your perceptions at the beginning of the day and do a follow-up journal at the end of the day for how it matched or did not match those perceptions.

## 3  Favorite Fragrance

*You may want to study biblical and extra-biblical sources to understand the greater meanings or specific ingredients of a particular fragrance. By studying something further in the natural realm, we will often be able to increase our prophetic insight.*

1. Divide into groups of three and have the youngest person share a favorite fragrance. Let the other two members of the group prophesy concerning the meaning of this favorite fragrance.

2. Now have the person to the left share a favorite fragrance and continue the same exercise until everyone has received a prophetic word.

3. For individual activation, ask the Lord, "What is my fragrance to You?" Write down the impressions the Lord gives you in this area.

# 4   Name That Tune

1. Have each person in the group pair up with another member. If that person were a song, what would the song be and why?

2. Circulate around the room pairing up with others in the same manner. Continue to move about the room until each person has shared a song with at least three other persons.

3. For individual activation, choose three family members. Ask the Lord for a song that represents each one prophetically. Write down the song and any additional reasoning or revelation you receive. Share it with your family member through a letter, email, or in person.

# 5   How God Touched Me

*Before you do this exercise, help the group become aware of the many ways they may experience God's touch. Explain that as they sense the Spirit of God, they might feel a change in a certain part of their body. For instance, their breathing or their mind may come to a state of rest or heightened awareness. Some may feel heaviness, fire or a burning sensation, a tingling, a peace, or the literal touch of a hand.*

1. Have the group close their eyes and be still before the Lord.

2. Pray over the members of the group that God would touch them in a tangible way.

3. Have the members of the group journal how God touched them.

4. Have the group dialogue with the Holy Spirit on what it might mean.

## 6 Sensitivity Journal

*This exercise is designed to build your sensitivity muscle for operating your senses in a Kingdom capacity. The five physical senses are touch, taste, smell, sight, and sound.*

1. During your times of personal devotional worship and prayer, journal the different sensations you experience and how they impacted you.

2. Keep track also of the various ways you encountered God through your senses as you went about your regular daily routine.

# Discussion and Reflection Questions

1. What was your previous perception of your natural senses—spiritual or unspiritual? Why?

_____

_____

2. Share experiences where your senses have accompanied or triggered a God-encounter. What did you see, hear, taste, smell, or touch? How did it impact you? If you have no recollection of this ever happening, ask God to remind you of any times where this type of perception occurred but you were not aware of it. Also share any perceptions you had today through activating your senses that brought prophetic encouragement to others.

_____

_____

_____

3. Read 1 John 1:1-4. How might these Scriptures apply to this chapter? What senses were part of the disciple's testimony? According to verse four, what was John's purpose for writing this declaration?

_____

_____

_____

_____

4. Which of your senses would you say is most exercised in spiritual perceptions? Which of your senses is least exercised as a spiritual perception? What is your workout plan for building your spiritual sensitivity with senses?

_____

_____

_____

_____

_____

_____

# Notes

Word of knowledge
partners with the prophetic to
stimulate faith.

# PROPHECY AND WORDS OF KNOWLEDGE

## CHAPTER FIVE

*Objective: Discover how the word of knowledge works together with the gift of prophecy.*

The manifestation gifts of the Spirit are described in the twelfth chapter of First Corinthians. Of course prophecy is one of the gifts listed there, but so is its twin sister—word of knowledge.

> *But to each one is given the manifestation of the Spirit for the common good. For to one is given the word of wisdom through the Spirit, and to another the word of knowledge according to the same Spirit* (vs. 7-8, NASB).

I call the gift of word of knowledge the twin sister of prophecy because they often work together. In my opinion, prophecy deals with potential truths present-to-future while word of knowledge deals with facts past-to-present.

I see at least three ways that the word of knowledge gift can partner with the prophetic gift.

## The Word of Knowledge Stimulates Faith

Word of knowledge is often used to stimulate faith. When a person shares knowledge about you that they have no way of knowing from a natural source, it creates an opportunity for faith to rise. Jesus used this gift on several occasions, one of the first of which was with Nathanael when Philip invited him to meet Jesus.

*Jesus saw Nathanael coming to him, and said of him, "Behold, an Israelite indeed, in whom there is no deceit!"*

*Nathanael said to Him, "How do you know me?" Jesus answered and said to him, "Before Philip called you, when you were under the fig tree, I saw you."*

*Nathanael answered Him, "Rabbi, You are the Son of God; You are the King of Israel."*

*Jesus answered and said to him, "Because I said to you that I saw you under the fig tree, do you believe? You will see greater things than these." And He said to him, "Truly, truly, I say to you, you will see the heavens opened and the angels of God ascending and descending on the Son of Man"* (John 1:47-51, NASB).

Notice here that Jesus told Nathanael something about him that had already happened—he was sitting under a fig tree when Philip called him. He also described Nathanael's character as "an Israelite in whom there is no deceit." Both of these bits of information were past-to-present; they were already true. These pieces of true information about Philip so stimulated his faith that he began to declare Jesus was the great teacher, the Son of God, and the King of Israel.

Jesus identifies that Nathanael's faith came directly from this gift of knowledge when He said, "Because I said to you that I saw you under the fig tree, do you believe?" Then Jesus follows the word of knowledge gift with the gift of prophecy and tells Nathanael what will happen in his future: "You will see greater things than these...you will see the heavens opened and the angels of God ascending and descending on the Son of Man."

This is just one of many examples of how Jesus used the word of knowledge and prophecy together.

## The Word of Knowledge Prepares the Way for the Prophetic

The word of knowledge is a breaker gift. It opens up a disbelieving or skeptical person to the realities of the Spirit.

Nathanael sounded skeptical about Jesus. He asked, "Can any good thing come out of Nazareth?"[21]

Philip wisely answered, "Come and see." Notice that Philip did not defend; he just invited the skeptic into an encounter with Jesus. When the unexplainable happened through the word of knowledge gift, Nathanael's skepticism transformed into faith. This faith opened the way for Nathanael to receive future information. The conversation moved from, "I saw..." to "You will see..." This is how the word of knowledge stimulates faith and opens the way for the prophetic in the realm of future information.

## The Word of Knowledge Provides Context

Another function of the word of knowledge gift is to provide context into a person's current or past situation. Context gives us confidence to deliver a prophetic word.

---

21  John 1:46.

Jesus demonstrated this with the woman at the well.

*The woman said to Him, "Sir, give me this water, so I will not be thirsty nor come all the way here to draw."*

*He said to her, "Go, call your husband and come here."*

*The woman answered and said, "I have no husband."*

*Jesus said to her, "You have correctly said, 'I have no husband;' for you have had five husbands, and the one whom you now have is not your husband; this you have said truly."*

*The woman said to Him, "Sir, I perceive that you are a prophet"* (John 4:15-19).

Jesus was ready to share His living water with the woman at the well but first she must deal with her sin. Notice that Jesus was not exposing her in front of others—this was a private conversation. The word of knowledge gift is not to embarrass, expose, or hang out someone's dirty laundry in front of others. Jesus' knowledge of her current circumstance was a context showing the potential obstacles to her receiving a greater blessing.

It does not take a prophet to see sin in a sinner; but it does take prophetic insight to see treasure in a life that is crowded with hurt, pain, and obstacles to blessing. You also do not have to actually be a prophet to see this treasure. Regardless of our giftings, every believer should be honoring the treasure in others.

### Mother

I remember one of the first times I used the word of knowledge gift in a public meeting. I was one of several speakers at a large youth camp. Even though the messages being delivered at the camp were excellent, I felt like the teenagers were mostly bored and zoning-out during the speaking. I prayed and asked the Lord to stir the atmosphere with spiritual gifts. All of sudden a blond young man stood out to me. I knew the Lord had a word for him so I asked God what it was. All that came to me was a single word, "Mother."

"What about his mother?" I asked in my spirit. "That's not exactly a prophetic word, Lord," I reminded God, "Everyone has had a mother at one point." Again, all that I heard was the same word, "Mother."

"Yes Lord," I said again in my spirit, "I have that part. But what are you saying about Mother?" The one word came again, "Mother." I think at this point I knew that the Lord would not give more until I was faithful with the little that I had. I asked the young man to stand up, and I told him I just heard one word over him, "Mother."

He looked down, and tears started flowing. Then the rest of the word came, "Oh, you are a twin," I said. The young man looked up and nodded. "You feel like your mom loves your brother more than you." Again the young man agreed.

"First of all, I feel like God is showing me that this is not true. Your mother loves you, but more than that, your Heavenly Father says that He loves you with an everlasting love..."

Beginning with these words I started prophesying over the young man. The meeting came alive with hope and expectation. Every student was sitting on the edge of his seat hoping for a word or wondering what would happen next.

Words of knowledge and prophecy created faith and broke open the way for God encounters.

In the above story, all three functions of the word of knowledge occurred. The immediate word of the wrong mindset he had about his mother gave me context for what the young man was dealing with. The accuracy of the word stimulated faith in the young man and in the whole room. Then I could speak to future things with the gift of prophecy and there was enough faith and credibility for everyone to believe.

This is an example of how a word of knowledge and prophecy often work together.

## How to Flow in the Word of Knowledge

Learning to flow in the word of knowledge is very similar to stirring up the prophetic in your life. Scripture invites us to "earnestly desire the greater gifts."[22]

*Pursue love, yet desire earnestly spiritual gifts, but especially that you may prophesy* (1 Corinthians 14:1, NASB).

The last verse of chapter twelve of First Corinthians and the first verse of chapter fourteen is our invitation to experience new spiritual gifts. We would not be encouraged to desire them if these new spiritual gifts were not available to all of us. After understanding this principle, the steps to receiving are very simple.

1. Believe that this gift is available to you.

2. Ask the Lord to give you this gift.

3. Receive the gift as an act of faith.

4. Exercise the gift as a demonstration of your faith.

---

22  1 Corinthians 12:31.

## Sense the Clues

I use the word *exercise* in the purest sense of the word. Remember the concept of taking your gift to the gymnasium and working it out?

In the same way, your word of knowledge gift may start very small with just a hint or a clue, but as you work it out and exercise it, the gift will get stronger, clearer, and more dynamic. The grace on the gift grows along with your faith and confidence.

Word of knowledge not only partners with the prophetic gift, but often shows up first in the area of healing. One of the easiest ways to begin to flow in the gift of word of knowledge is when you sense God showing you someone who needs healing in their body.

## Sympathetic Pains

Impressions of words of knowledge can come to you in many forms. It can come as a sympathetic pain where you actually feel the pain of others in your physical body with no causation or previous pain in that area.

### Kidney Pain

We were just getting ready to begin the preaching part of our pastors' conference in Northern India. The bright colors worn by the native Indians looked like a field of wild flowers. My senior pastors' wife came to me weak with pain and said she needed to return to the hotel because her kidneys were hurting so bad. I asked her what happened or if she had any previous kidney trouble. She answered that nothing had happened and she had no history of kidney problems.

"Do you think this could be a word of knowledge?" I asked.

"It feels like it's mine," she answered, "but, let's see."

We got permission to interrupt the senior pastor who was already well into his message.

"Is anyone here suffering from severe kidney pain right now?" we inquired. Fourteen people came forward, one of which had tumors on her kidneys and was currently experiencing excruciating pain.

All fourteen were healed, and our pastor's wife who had the sympathetic pains became totally pain free.

## Gut Feelings

Along with an empathetic perception of pain or discomfort, the word of knowledge can also occur simply as an impression or a knowing in your "gut."

Twelve times in Scripture Jesus healed someone when He was "moved with compassion." The Greek root for this phrase "moved with compassion" comes from the word "gut" or "intestines."

Sometimes you just know something in the depths of your being. You do not know how you know it, but if you act on what you are sensing, people will be powerfully touched.

## Head Pain

I was teaching in Southern California at a healing school. People gathered from nearly twenty churches in this beach paradise to pursue a greater understanding of the gifts of healing. During the meeting, I felt like there was someone present who had a sharp pain across their forehead just above their eyebrows and running parallel to their eyes. I was not feeling the pain myself; I just knew it in my "knower." A man in his early thirties came forward and said that this described the exact pain he had suffered for many years. After I ministered to him briefly, all of the pain left.

What God reveals, we have confidence that He heals. Our faith, and the faith of those who receive healing, often increases through the operation of the word of knowledge gift.

## Take a Risk

People always ask the question, "But what if I am wrong and no one responds?" My friend Bill Johnson says that the worst thing that can happen is nothing. On the other hand, you could experience a miracle.

### Non-Responders

I took a team from our supernatural school on a tour of smaller churches in the Nevada desert. One night we were ministering words of knowledge at a gathering for several churches in Nevada's capital city. I asked the students to be as detailed as they could with any words of knowledge. The first student called out a stomach surgery that had gone wrong and now the pain had worsened. No one responded. The next student called out a trauma injury to the back of the head. No one responded. The third student called out a severe pain and lack of mobility in both knees. No one responded. By the time the fourth student gave his word of knowledge, people began to respond to the words that were being called out.

After a time of releasing healing, we asked for testimonies. The first testimony was from a woman who had a failed stomach surgery and now all her pain was gone. The second testimony came from a church leader who had suffered a hit to the head with a metal object when he was younger. Now his head was tingling in the spot of the trauma and his whole head felt lighter. The third testimony was from a woman flexing her knees up and down demonstrating her new pain free mobility. Other testimonies came as well, but I had to laugh that even though no one responded to those first three words of knowledge, God still healed those exact conditions.

Word of knowledge often pairs with both healing and prophecy to stimulate faith, open the door for increased ministry, and give a context to what people are going through.

# Recommended Prophetic Activations

## 1 Healing Words

*Ask the Lord to manifest words of knowledge for healing in your group. Encourage everyone to be sensitive to sympathetic pains within their own bodies or impressions of what the Lord is focusing on for healing.*

1. Have each member of the group share any words of knowledge they are getting for physical healing.

2. Ask those who responded with the condition called—or they need healing in that area—to stand up.

3. Have the group member who received the word of knowledge minister healing to those who have stood.

4. Command the pain or condition to go, and release the healing virtue of God.

5. After praying for the person to be healed, ask if there is a change in their condition.

6. Give some time for testimonies of healing at the end of the ministry.

## 2 Treasure Hunts

*Kevin Dedmon, one of the pastors at Bethel Church in Redding, California, has made famous the concept of using words of knowledge for evangelistic treasure hunts.[23] Many people have been saved, healed, or greatly touched by God's love through this kind of compassionate prophetic evangelism.*

1. In a group of three to five people, ask God for words of knowledge that give specifics about people's names, clothing, appearance, and prayer needs. Also, ask God for words of knowledge about locations and other unusual things.

2. Write these clues down on a paper. This is your "treasure map."

3. The team will travel to the location on the map to find these "treasures" of people according to the specific clues received.

4. When the person who fits the clues is found, show this person the treasure map.

5. Ask the person if they would like prayer for the specific need.

6. For individual activation, see #27 "Personal Treasure Hunt" in the Appendix of Prophetic Activations.

## 3  In-House Treasure Hunt

*If your group is big enough, you can do an in-house treasure hunt. This activation needs sufficient time for everyone to search for the "treasure" in the room or on campus.*

1. Without looking around the room, ask God to show you factors that describe a person (i.e., name, clothing color, and prayer needs). Write your clues down on a piece of paper. This will be your "treasure map."

---

23  *The Ultimate Treasure Hunt* by Kevin Dedmon explains this concept fully.

2. Release the group to go find the people in the room who match the clues on their treasure maps.

3. When you find the person who matches your clues, show them what was written down and offer to pray for them.

4. After sufficient time, ask how many found someone who matched their clues. Allow some time for testimonies of healing or other significant encounters that happened during the treasure hunt.

5. If there are any participants who did not find the one who matched their clues, encourage them to be watching for that person throughout the rest of the day.

## 4   Family Ties

*This is a great way to practice receiving words of knowledge.*

1. Divide your group into pairs. Have them sit in chairs facing one another. It is best to pair up with someone whom you do not know very well.

2. Ask the Lord to give you information about a person in your partner's family. You might see a name, a face, a hair color, a city, a specific situation or need. Share the information with your partner and get feedback on its accuracy. If you appear to miss it, try again with different information. You can rotate pairs two or three times to exercise your "faith muscle" for a word of knowledge.

3. If you are processing this activation on your own, choose three friends, classmates or co-workers. Ask the Lord for the same types of family information and needs. Write down and date the information you receive. Contact the persons, or wait for an appropriate time to begin a conversation about the person's family. You could say something like, "I was praying for you the other day and wrote

these things down about a family member of yours." Show them the paper and offer to pray for them and their family.

## 5 Spiritual Caller ID

*This is a fun way to practice the word of knowledge and exercise your faith at home.*

1. When the home phone or cell phone rings, try to predict who it is and what the caller wants. Use your "internal caller ID" and practice this until it becomes common to receive the correct information.

2. You can do the same thing when there is a knock at your door. Expect that God will show you who is there through exercising a word of knowledge.

## 6 Word of Knowledge Journal

*Every day can be a personal treasure hunt. In your devotional time, you can journal simple things that you expect will happen during the day.*

1. Who will you meet?

2. Who will call?

3. What things will happen?

4. What are the needs you must be prepared to meet today?

5. Ask yourself: What Scriptures or encouragements have I recently received that I can have on hand to minister to the needs of others?

Write down your clues or expectations for the day and journal the results before bed or sometime the following day.

## 7 Social Networks and Words of Knowledge

*In the same way that you receive words of knowledge for healing and treasure hunts, you can use email, cell phone text, or social network sites to practice words of knowledge.*

*Ask the Lord how you can minister to a friend in need today.*

1. What names, faces, or places come before you?

2. What are the needs?

3. How can you minister to them?

4. With what God gives you, create a cell phone text, email, or social network posting to share this encouragement with your friends.

## 8 The Envelope Please

*This activation is for those who are well-exercised in receiving a word of knowledge, but it is good practice for the inexperienced as well.*

1. From the internet, print off ten photographs of celebrities that everyone in your group would know. These might include politicians, actors, musicians, or religious figures.

2. Place each picture inside a separate envelope. Then seal the envelopes and give each a number from one to ten.

3. Have each member of your group take out a sheet of paper and

number it from one to ten. Leave approximately three empty lines between each number to include additional information.

4. Pass these numbered envelopes around the group. Without looking inside, each group member will try to get a name, a gender, a hair color, a clothing item or other significant fact about the person whose photo is inside the envelope. Write up to three clues for each envelope.

5. When everyone has received all ten envelopes and has written down clues for each, open the envelopes and reveal the pictures.

6. Have group members check how many details they got correct concerning the celebrity inside the envelope.

7. For individual activation, ask a friend or family member to prepare the photos and envelopes for you.

Don't be discouraged if you do not get many correct at first, as this is one of the more advanced activation exercises.

## Discussion and Reflection Questions

1. What other Scriptures or Bible stories can you think of that reveal the operation of the word of knowledge? (Example: 2 Kings 6:12.)

   _____

   _____

2. What is your previous experience with the gift of word of knowledge? Think of your greatest breakthrough using the word of knowledge gift. Have you ever "missed" a word of knowledge? Briefly share your positive and challenging experiences with the group.

   _____

   _____

3. Read Hebrews 4:15:

   *For we do not have a high priest who is unable to sympathize with our weaknesses, but we have one who has been tempted in every way, just as we are—yet was without sin.*

   The word "weakness" here can mean "feebleness of health or sickness, frailty, weak understanding of a thing, weak restraint of corrupt desires, ability to bear trials and troubles."

   A. How does this passage potentially relate to word of knowledge gift?

   _____

   _____

B. What does it mean that Jesus, our High Priest, can sympathize with our weaknesses?

_____

_____

C. What is your exercise plan to increase the grace and faith for activating the word of knowledge in your life?

_____

_____

# Notes

The abundance of God's thoughts
toward each person gives
us confidence to
speak prophetic encouragement
at any moment.

# PREPARING FOR SUDDENLIES

## CHAPTER SIX

*Objective: Strengthen your ability to be instantly ready to release prophetic encouragement.*

We do not always have time to prepare or deliver a long prophetic word. Sometimes the window to share a prophetic encouragement with someone is sudden and short. The following Scriptures encourage us to be prepared in and out of season and to stir up the gifts that are within us.

> *Preach the word; be ready in season and out of season; reprove, rebuke, exhort, with great patience and instruction* (2 Timothy 4:2, NASB).

*Do not neglect the spiritual gift within you, which was bestowed on you through prophetic utterance with the laying on of hands by the presbytery* (1 Timothy 4:14, NASB).

*For this reason I remind you to kindle afresh the gift of God which is in you through the laying on of my hands* (2 Timothy 1:6, NASB).

# Being Prepared Out of Season

How do you prepare for sudden unexpected encounters? How do you stir up or kindle your own gift of prophecy? I think the answers to these questions start with your belief system. What we believe determines what we expect and how we live.

Here are two belief systems that help me always be ready to share a prophetic word. I think they will help you too.

## God's Thoughts Towards Us are Innumerable

If we believe God has one specific thought or prophetic word toward people, there is pressure to find that one thing that God is truly saying in the moment. It often feels like a one-in-a-million chance. But if we consider that God's thoughts toward any human being at any given moment are as many as the sands of the seas, then it removes anxiety. I like to picture myself walking down a beach. All the grains of sand are like thoughts God has concerning the person I am speaking to. In prophetic ministry, it is kind of like reaching down to grab a handful of the sand and simply sharing the few things that are in my hand. When I realize that God has many wonderful things to speak about any one person, the abundance of His thoughts gives me confidence to be ready.

*How precious also are Your thoughts to me, O God! How vast is the sum of them! If I should count them, they would outnumber the sand. When I awake, I am still with You* (Psalm 139:17-18, NASB).

## God's Gifts Remain in Me

My confidence to always be ready also comes from the strength of His word and presence. God is always with me. His anointing is always in me. His gifts are always on me, and He will never take them away.

How can I feel unprepared in any circumstance if I hold to these promises of His Word?

> *For God's gifts and his call are irrevocable* (Romans 11:29).

> *But you have an anointing from the Holy One, and all of you know the truth...As for you, the anointing you received from him remains in you...*(1 John 2:20, 27).

Readiness also comes with practice. Remember doing addition and subtraction drills when you were a child? My mom would hold up flash cards, and the goal was to read and answer the equation as quickly as possible.

The same exercise is true in music. A young musician might practice one musical phrase or scale over and over again. At first, playing the scale requires all of the person's concentration, but through deep practice, playing the music becomes second nature.

One of the goals for this chapter is to do some deep practice speed drills that will help us be ready to share prophetic encouragement on demand.

# Recommended Prophetic Activations

## 1  Back to Back

*This exercise works really well in a larger group. Continue alternating groups until each one has delivered back-to-back prophecies over at least three different people.*

1. Have half of your group stand in a line with their backs facing the rest of the group.

2. Now ask the other half of the group to choose one person in the line to stand behind. Stand facing the back of the person you have chosen.

3. When the group leader gives the signal, the first group will turn around and face the person standing behind them. The person who turned around will have only 60 seconds to deliver a word of prophetic encouragement.

4. Next have the second group turn their backs to the first group. Everyone in the first group switches places and stands facing the back of the person they have chosen.

5. On the signal, the second group will turn and face the members of the first group in their new positions and deliver a 60-second prophetic word.

## 2   Phone-a-Friend Prophecy

*Make this exercise a regular practice of sending prophetic words and encouragement to friends and family through email, social networks, and cell phone text messages.*

1. Choose someone from your cell phone contacts, social network, or email contacts list to prophesy over.

2. Because this form of communication is characteristically short, condense your prophetic words down to as few lines as possible. You can start the message with something like, "I was thinking of you today and felt like I heard…"

## 3   Popcorn Prophecy

*This activation trains you in speed, listening and interacting with one another by saying something meaningful in a very short and concise way.*

*One person after another "pops off" a prophetic sentence that relates to the person seated and relates to what was said by the one who spoke just before.*

1. Find a volunteer and seat them in a chair placed in the middle of a circle. The rest of the group will stand around the person seated.

2. Each person in the group will speak only one sentence of prophetic encouragement to the one in the middle. Do not share a second pop-prophecy word until each member has spoken.

3. Keep this prophetic flow going by tagging onto the previous comment in rapid succession.

# 4    Thirty-Second Drill

*This activation exercises our ability to prophesy quickly and briefly so that we are always prepared to give an encouraging word.*

1. Number your group 1-2-1-2-1-2, etc., until everyone has received a number.

2. Have the group stand. Announce that in a moment the signal will be given and those with the number one will have 30 seconds to prophesy over the number two on their right. (The persons on the end of the row may need to cross the room.)

3. Give the signal, "Go!" Watch the clock and announce when there are only ten seconds left.

4. At the 30-second mark, call "Stop!"

5. Now with no delay, announce that the twos will also have 30 seconds to prophesy over the number ones on their right. This is a different person than the one who just prophesied over them. Call "Go!"

6. Give the warning when ten seconds remain. After 30 seconds are up, call "Stop!"

7. Now have the number ones prophesy to a number two directly behind them. (Back rows can move to prophesy over the twos in the front row.)

8. Keep using different configurations of the ones and twos until every person has had several opportunities using the thirty-second drill.

## Discussion and Reflection Questions

1. Have you ever missed an opportunity for prophetic encouragement and regretted it later? Have you ever had a sudden moment of prophetic inspiration for someone? Share your worst or best experience with the group.

   _____

   _____

2. What past beliefs have made it most difficult to be ready to prophesy in and out of season? What beliefs help you most to be ready to share prophetic encouragement with others?

   _____

   _____

3. How do you stir up your own gift of prophecy? What things help you access or ignite your gift?

   _____

   _____

4. Read Acts 8:26-40. Even though Philip did not deliver a "prophetic word" in this account, how is this an example of hearing God and responding quickly?

   _____

   _____

5. Read the following verses in the NIV focusing on the word "prepared":

1 Corinthians 2:9, Ephesians 2:10, 2 Timothy 4:2, and 1 Peter 3:15. What are the things that God has prepared for you? Where are the areas that you are to prepare yourself? How are you preparing yourself for the things that God has prepared for you?

_____

_____

_____

_____

_____

_____

_____

# Notes

Giving, combined
with prophetic insight, yields
exponentially great and powerful
results in both the giver and
the receiver.

# PROPHETIC GIVING

## CHAPTER SEVEN

*Objective: Discover how giving with a prophetic leading can have a profound impact on others.*

In previous chapters, we have explored some of the manifestation "gifts of the Spirit" mentioned in First Corinthians chapter twelve. Romans chapter twelve also contains a listing of gifts which are sometimes referred to as the "motivational gifts."

Among this listing of the motivational gifts, we find both the gift of prophecy and the gift of contributing to the needs of others.

> *We have different gifts, according to the grace given to us. If a man's gift is prophesying, let him use it in proportion to his faith... if it is contributing to the needs of others, let him give generously...* (Romans 12:6, 8).

In the book of Second Corinthians, believers are encouraged to excel in the grace of giving just as we do in faith, knowledge, and speech.

*But just as you excel in everything—in faith, in speech, in knowledge, in complete earnestness and in your love for us—see that you also excel in this grace of giving* (2 Corinthians 8:7).

In Chapter Five we learned how pairing other gifts, like the word of knowledge, with the gift of prophecy greatly increases both gifts' impact and results.

In the same way, giving can partner with prophecy and yield exponentially great and powerful results in both the giver and the receiver.

### Generous Prophetic Provision

It was my first foreign mission trip and the final organizational meeting started in ten minutes. Our money was due, and I was still $856.11 short of being able to go. I had hoped for a miracle of some kind that morning in church, but none had come. Resigning myself to the thought that I would go next time, I began to climb the stairwell leading to the meeting room where I would drop out of the trip.

All of a sudden, an elderly woman stopped me at the foot of the stairs and said that she wanted to do "a little something for my trip." She pushed an envelope into my hand that held some type of greeting card. I thanked her and let her know that I did not think I would have enough money for this trip, and that if this was the case, I promised to return her gift. She smiled politely and walked away.

As I began to climb the next flight of stairs, I opened the card. One hundred...two hundred...wow! Five hundred...eight hundred...I kept counting. That card held eight hundred and fifty-six dollars!

I was shocked. Balances were kept strictly confidential, and I had told absolutely no one the amount of money I still needed for the trip. (I added in the extra eleven cents needed myself.)

The gift from this kind, elderly woman was not only a large and generous amount, but she had prophetically given exactly what I needed. Receiving the money in this way not only confirmed that I was to go on the trip, but it taught me how clearly people can hear God in the area of giving.

# Three Types of Prophetic Giving

Prophetic giving can be expressed in many different ways, but here are three types of prophetic giving that can get us started.

## Giving a Need Gift

Giving specifically and strategically to a need is a powerful demonstration of supernatural grace and love. Giving includes more than money. Prophetic giving can be as simple as sharing a pencil at school, taking a cake to a next door neighbor, or paying for grocery items for the person behind you in line. The need or amount can be known or unknown. Prophetic giving is characterized by an inward prompting of the Holy Spirit along with the grace and ability to act upon a specific need.

One of my favorite stories that illustrate prophetically giving to a need came from the following story.

## Gallon of Milk

Following a Bible study late one night, a young man felt strangely prompted to stop and buy a gallon of milk as he made his way home. Taking the jug of milk back to his car, he felt prompted to take a different route home.

Halfway home, the young man again followed an inward leading to turn the opposite direction from his route. He pulled up in front of a stranger's house and felt led to take the jug of milk to the front door. Nervously, he approached the front door while trying to work up some explanation for why he was standing there with a jug of milk.

As he rang the bell, a man's voice yelled out, "Who is it? What do you want?" The door opened and the young man quickly thrust out the gallon of milk, "Here, I brought this for you."

With tears streaming down his face, the man said, "I was just praying and asking God to show me how to get some milk for my babies." At that moment, his wife came to the door holding a child on her hip. "Are you an angel? I just asked God to send an angel with some milk."

The young man reached into his wallet and pulled out all the money he had on him and put it in the man's hand.

## Giving a Seed Gift

A seed gift refers to sowing into something you believe in. This type of gift is not characterized by the size of the need but the focus of the dream, vision, or purpose. You may want to sow a gift into someone's marriage, a family vacation, a ministry or business start-up, or any number of things that people are passionately pursuing. Often people sow a seed gift into an area where they would like to see a return some day.

> *Remember this: Whoever sows sparingly will also reap sparingly, and whoever sows generously will also reap generously... Now he who supplies seed to the sower and bread for food will also supply and increase your store of seed and will enlarge the harvest of your righteousness (2 Corinthians 9:6,10).*

### The Food-Filled Freezer

My wife and I had just purchased our first house in California. Arriving home from work one day, my wife met me with some surprising news. A generous man in the church had bought us a large stand-up freezer and filled it with six months' worth of meat. I walked out to the garage to see the amazing gift and then called the giver. He explained that he never had enough meat to eat as a child and wanted our kids to always have enough. He also said that he and his wife were hoping to buy a new house and so they were sowing this gift into ours. Soon, this couple miraculously was able to move into their new dream home.

It is not wrong to hope for a harvest return when you sow a seed gift. That is why it is called sowing. No farmer plants seed in the ground without expecting to reap a bountiful harvest. Sowing in faith and love into the lives of others is one of the ways that we demonstrate our faith.

## Giving a Love Gift

A love gift is not based upon need or a specific cause; it is given as a statement of love, honor, appreciation, and blessing. Love gifts can also be prophetic in nature.

### The Generous $100-Tip

A minister friend was visiting from Australia and received terrible service at a local restaurant. The waitress was rude, the food was served cold, and the order was not quite right. At the end of his meal, my friend left a one hundred dollar tip and walked out to his car. As he was getting into his car, the waitress came running out to the parking lot with the one hundred dollar bill in hand.

"Sir!' she cried. "You left this at the table."

"Yes, that's your tip," he replied.

The waitress was shocked. "But why would you...I was so rude..." she confessed.

The minister replied, "I just figured you must be having a really rough day and needed someone to bless you. You know, God loves you even when you're having a bad day."

With those words she broke down, and the minister was able to pray with her as she gave her life to God.

Love does not need a reason to express itself, but a love gift can have an intended purpose.


## A Creative Prophetic Love Gift

Michele is a painter and poet who also works as a delivery nurse at the local hospital. Her mother does not yet know the Lord and resists most conversations about spiritual things.

Michele had recently self-published a book of her poems and gave it to her mom along with a picture that she had painted. Her mother would often sit in front of the painting and just stare at it feeling waves of peace overtake her. Reading the poems would often have the same effect.

When her mother went to her monthly medical appointment, a strange thing occurred. The crippling foot condition that she had suffered from for years was disappearing. The doctor asked what she had done different with her feet or her diet—he was looking for some catalyst for the change. Michele's mom attributed the physical change to the painting and poems that her daughter had given her.

These gifts were acting like windows of heaven releasing God's love, power, and peace over Michele's mother.

## The Breaker Tool

One of the powers of a prophetic love gift is that it can carry the blessing, virtue, and intent of the one who gave it. Just like something that is cursed can open the way for darkness, something that is blessed opens the way for light.

Paul's handkerchiefs and aprons carried that power and blessing.

> *So that even handkerchiefs and aprons that had touched him were taken to the sick, and their illnesses were cured and the evil spirits left them* (Acts 19:12).

This chapter explored how prophetic giving can take many forms—giving prophetically to a need, through a seed, or through a love gift—and that each has its own powerful impact.

Proverbs 18:6 tells us:

> *A gift opens the way for the giver and ushers him into the presence of the great.*

A prophetic gift can be a breaker tool to break down the walls of resistance and open opportunities to manifest the King and His Kingdom. Prophetic giving can demonstrate the love and power of God in a practical way. As a seed, prophetic giving can release exponential increase and limitless possibilities. Prophetic insights give clarity and effectual action to the overwhelming ocean of human need by focusing our giving in a more strategic way.

The following activations are designed to help you experience a diversity of expressions in the joy of prophetic giving.

# Recommended Prophetic Activations

## 1 See the Needs

*Remember that a gift does not always have to be monetary or expensive to make a powerful impact.*

1. Write down a list of people you are regularly interacting with and consider their specific needs.

2. Pray over the list and ask the Lord if He would have you give anything towards one of these needs.

## 2 Pay the Way

*If we watch and prepare for prophetic opportunities, we will see a huge increase in divine appointments and supernatural assignments. A fun way to practice prophetic giving is to make a habit out of paying the way for others. Here are a few ideas.*

1. Plan to pay the way of the car behind you at the toll booth.

2. Pay for the groceries of a young mother or a widow at the store.

3. Purchase tickets for the person behind you in line at the movie theater.

4. Buy an extra grocery item to give away.

5. Place folded dollar bills between jars of baby food in the baby food aisle at the grocery store.

## 3   Prophetic Gift Exchange

*This exercise, which is activated by a small prophetic gift, can make a great impact on the one receiving it.*

1. Prepare a small gift for a friend or family member that is a trigger for a prophetic encouragement.

2. Write out the word or share it with the person as you give the gift.

## 4   Atmospheric Gift

*Ask God to show you a gift that would be meaningful to the one receiving it. Try to choose a gift with no obvious spiritual meaning. Choose something that the person would see every day, such as a picture, a sculpture, a piece of jewelry, or favorite clothing item. It should be a gift that they would put in a prominent place somewhere in their house. Make sure the gift you purchase is something that the person would really enjoy.*

1. Write out the name of a family member, friend, or co-worker who does not yet know the Lord.

2. Purchase the item and take it to your prayer closet. Lay your hands on the item and pray over it often. Soak it with presence while you worship and commune with the Lord. Ask the Lord to anoint the item like He did the handkerchiefs and aprons that Paul had touched.[24]

---

24  Acts 19:12.

3. When you give the gift to this designated person, don't say anything about your spiritual preparation time over it or its prophetic meaning. Just share the gift in the spirit of love and watch to see what happens.

## 5 Prophetic Sowing

*Identify a dream or vision that you have for your future. Perhaps you are hoping to start a business, buy a home, or go on vacation. It could be a relational dream you have had, like finding a mate or having a child. It could also be a mission-focused dream of starting an orphanage, a non-profit organization, or ministering in another country. See how God would have you give a financial gift as an opportunity to prophetically sow into your own dream or vision.*

1. Write down your dream or vision. If you have more than one of these types of dreams or visions, then write three to five of the most prominent on a piece of paper or in a journal.

2. Pray about how God might have you sow a gift into someone who is doing something similar to your own dream.

3. Pray over the gift or the amount, and tell the Lord that you are joyfully planting this as a seed, prayerfully expecting a harvest from God's goodness. You may want to put more than one seed in the ground.

## 6 Prophetic Gift Exchange

*This activation trains you to see the prophetic meaning behind a gift.*

1. Print the names of your group members on cards or small slips of paper.

2. Pass out the name cards to each member of the group.

3. Have your group members return the following week with an item from home or an inexpensive purchased item that prophetically represents something they feel the Lord is speaking into the life of the person whose name they received.

4. Gather your group in a circle and have them present their gifts one-by-one along with what the Lord is saying through that gift.

## Discussion and Reflection Questions

1. Have you ever received a gift that had prophetic meaning to it? Briefly share your story with the group?

   _____

   _____

2. What is the primary difference between giving to a need and giving a seed?

   _____

   _____

3. Read 2 Corinthians 8:7 again. What does it mean to excel in the grace of giving?

   _____

   _____

4. What are some of the ways that God demonstrates that He is a generous giver? Search the phrase "I will give" in Scripture to reveal how often and in what ways God gives to man. Has God ever given you a gift that had prophetic meaning to you?

   _____

   _____

5. What is the easiest area for you to be generous in? What is the hardest area for you to be generous in? Why do you think that is? What should you do about it?

_____

_____

6. What action plan can you set up to be more prophetically active in your giving?

_____

_____

# Notes

Prophetic actions in the
earthly realm release a powerful
shift in the spirit realm.

# PROPHETIC ACTS

## CHAPTER EIGHT

*Objective: Make a huge practical impact through a
small prophetic action.*

The Bible is full of small prophetic actions that had huge practical impact. Perhaps none is better known than the hands of Moses against the Amalekites.

> *As long as Moses held up his hands, the Israelites were winning, but whenever he lowered his hands, the Amalekites were winning. When Moses' hands grew tired, they took a stone and put it under him and he sat on it. Aaron and Hur held his hands up—one on one side, one on the other—so that his hands remained steady till sunset. So Joshua overcame the Amalekite army with the sword* (Exodus 17:11-13).

This story takes us to a mysterious area of the prophetic. Why do certain actions release realities in the spiritual realm? I do not know that I have heard a great answer to that question, but there is no doubt it does happen.

Here is another example from the final days of the double-portion prophet Elisha.

> Elisha said, "Get a bow and some arrows," and he did so. "Take the bow in your hands," he said to the king of Israel. When he had taken it, Elisha put his hands on the king's hands. "Open the east window," he said, and he opened it. "Shoot!" Elisha said, and he shot. "The LORD's arrow of victory, the arrow of victory over Aram!" Elisha declared. "You will completely destroy the Arameans at Aphek."
>
> Then he said, "Take the arrows," and the king took them. Elisha told him, "Strike the ground." He struck it three times and stopped. The man of God was angry with him and said, "You should have struck the ground five or six times; then you would have defeated Aram and completely destroyed it. But now you will defeat it only three times" (2 Kings 13:15-19).

## The Gospel of John

Many years ago I was in a time of intense prayer for the nation of Haiti. As I prayed I felt a spirit of fear come over me. The enemy began to lie in my ear that if I prayed for Haiti, the voodoo spirits would make sure that my family was attacked and my children molested. At first I hesitated to pray on, and then a spirit of boldness and confidence hit me.

I grabbed a small wooden box that had been hand carved in Haiti. The box was just big enough to hold a small paperback copy of the book of John that I had in my office. I placed the Gospel inside the box and proclaimed, "The blessings of God are stronger than any curse. I proclaim that the Gospel will go forth to every home in Haiti." (Notice that I didn't confront the voodoo spirit but rather proclaimed the blessings of God through my words and prophetic action.)

I prayed along this line for quite some time. Later that month I read an article in a mission magazine about a group that was taking the book of John door-to-door to every house in the nation of Haiti. My prayers had been literally answered through that small prophetic act.

## Prophetic Actions as Intercession

The first two biblical examples we read and my own personal story relate to what is often called "prophetic intercession." In this type of intercession, the will of God is released in the earth through the movements or actions of someone directed by God. The action or movement in the earthly realm releases a specific blessing or reality in the spirit realm.

### Incense in the Foundation

When building The Mission church in Vacaville, California, the leadership was prompted to perform several acts of prophetic intercession in the foundation of the building. Many of the walls and concrete were coated with handwritten Scriptures before they were plastered or treated. The prayer room has a huge bull's-eye target painted under the carpet. There are gemstones buried in the foundation representing various truths.

Recently, I was doing a session in our 24/7 worship room when the senior leader's wife and head intercessor started getting very excited. I was singing a song about our praise rising as incense, and I could see them both sniffing the air with expressions of awe and wonder. After worship they told me what had happened.

At the very moment these two ladies were in a conversation about how they had buried burning incense in the foundation of this very room—ten years before it was even known that it would one day become a dedicated 24/7 worship and prayer room!—I began to sing a song about worship being like incense to the Lord. The ladies became very excited, when suddenly, they began to literally smell sweet incense filling the room. This incense manifestation, the timing of the conversation, and the song about incense being sung, was a confirmation to us that this room had indeed always been meant for the purpose of unending prayer and worship. We were all greatly encouraged.

## Prophetic Actions as Communication

God is not bound to audible language; it may not even be His preferred way of speaking. The prophetic can be powerfully released through actions and movements as the mode of communication. This was a primary way of prophetic ministry for the Old Testament prophet Ezekiel. Many of Ezekiel's messages were conveyed through prophetic actions. Here is an example using Ezekiel's hair as part of the message from God.

> *"Now, son of man, take a sharp sword and use it as a barber's razor to shave your head and your beard. Then take a set of scales and divide up the hair. When the days of your siege come to an end, burn a third of the hair with fire inside the city. Take a third and strike it with the sword all around the city. And scatter a third to the wind. For I will pursue them with drawn sword. But take a few strands of hair and tuck them away in the folds of your garment. Again, take a few of these and throw them into the fire and burn them up. A fire will spread from there to the whole house of Israel* (Ezekiel 5:1-4).

This method of prophetic ministry is not limited to Old Testament prophets. In the New Testament the prophet Agabus did a prophetic action with Paul's belt to deliver the word of the Lord.

> *After we had been there a number of days, a prophet named Agabus came down from Judea. Coming over to us, he took Paul's belt, tied his own hands and feet with it and said, "The Holy Spirit says, 'In this way the Jews of Jerusalem will bind the owner of this belt and will hand him over to the Gentiles'"* (Acts 21:10-11).

Timing, good boundaries, and sensitivity to the Holy Spirit are absolute keys to this powerful mode of communication. Be sure to watch for many of the other examples of prophetic actions as communication in Scripture.

## Prophetic Actions as Demonstration

Prophetic actions can also be demonstrations of faith or obedience. In both the Old and New Testaments, there are examples of persons being healed as they responded obediently to a specific command.

> *Elisha sent a messenger to say to him, "Go, wash yourself seven times in the Jordan, and your flesh will be restored and you will be cleansed."... So he went down and dipped himself in the Jordan seven times, as the man of God had told him, and his flesh was restored and became clean like that of a young boy* (2 Kings 5:10,14).

> *As he was going into a village, ten men who had leprosy met him. They stood at a distance and called out in a loud voice, "Jesus, Master, have pity on us!" When he saw them, he said, "Go, show yourselves to the priests." And as they went, they were cleansed* (Luke 17:12-14).

In both the Old and New Testament cases of a leprous skin condition, neither of the subjects experienced healing until they performed a specific action of faith and obedience. This action was a prophetic demonstration of their belief that resulted in their healing.

A prophetic demonstration of faith can be performed by the person who is receiving the healing or by the one who is ministering the blessing.

### Pulling out Flaming Darts

I was speaking at a school of the supernatural in Singapore one summer. One of the students had chronic shoulder pain for many months. I felt the Lord prompt me to reach down and prophetically pull a flaming dart out of that shoulder region.[25] Immediately all of the pain left and she was totally healed.

The prophetic action in the natural realm released the spiritual reality of healing.

Other miracles besides healing can be prompted by prophetic action. The miracle of provision and multiplication were also prompted by prophetic actions in both the Old and New Testaments.

*Elisha said, "Go around and ask all your neighbors for empty jars. Don't ask for just a few. Then go inside and shut the door behind you and your sons. Pour oil into all the jars, and as each is filled, put it to one side." She left him and afterward shut the door behind her and her sons. They brought the jars to her and she kept pouring. When all the jars were full, she said to her son, "Bring me another one." But he replied. "There is not a jar left." Then the oil stopped flowing. She went and told the man of God, and he said, "Go sell the oil and pay your debts. You and your sons can live on what is left"* (2 Kings 4:3-7).

---

25  Ephesians 6:16, Psalm 64:3, Proverbs 26:18-19.

*But so that we may not offend them, go to the lake and throw out your line. Take the first fish you catch; open its mouth and you will find a four-drachma coin. Take it and give it to them for my tax and yours* (Matthew 17:27).

Miracles, healing, and multiplication through prophetic actions and obedience are still being reported today.

## Two Hundred Bowls of Soup

Heidi Baker, missionary to Mozambique, tells the story of not having enough food for their two hundred orphans. As they were praying and thanking the Lord for their next meal, a neighbor stopped by with a bowl of soup.

The soup was sufficient enough to feed Heidi's immediate family only. What Heidi did next stands as a true prophetic demonstration of her faith and obedience. She had all two hundred children sit down with their bowls and give thanks to the Lord.

From the pot of soup made for her small family, Heidi began to dish out portions into each individual bowl until all two hundred bowls had been filled with soup, including the soup bowls of her immediate family.[26]

The prophetic actions of intercession, communication, and demonstration—even in the smallest measure—are sure to release a spiritual shift and blessing in your region.

---

26   *Always Enough: God's Miraculous Provision Among the Poorest Children on Earth*, by Rolland and Heidi Baker.

# Recommended Prophetic Activations

### 1 Healing Through Prophetic Acts

*As in the biblical example found in 2 Kings 13, this exercise must be performed with faith and definite passion. Focus on the center of the prayer target's pain. Remember to ask the Lord for sight or perception of where the pain is focused.*

1. Ask your group how many of them have shoulder, back, or neck pain that has no apparent cause. Find out how many of them feel the cause could be a dart or arrow of the enemy. Have those persons come forward and form a line across the front of the room.

2. Ask for volunteers from your group to come up, and with a prophetic action, remove the arrows. Remind them to firmly take hold of the invisible arrow and give it a strong yank.

3. After performing this prophetic act, ask those who had the pain if they notice any change. Some should feel an immediate difference in their pain level; others may have a more natural root or a need that requires another approach to see their full healing.

4. Celebrate all those who are healed, and thank the Lord.

### 2 Prophetic Movements

*Worship times provide another great opportunity to explore the power of prophetic actions.*

1. Turn the lights low in the room so that people will be less self-conscious.

2. Play music that has a prophetic or intercessory tone from a public sound system or portable music player.

3. Invite group members to respond physically to the music without singing. Some may want to dance, march, lift their arms, or bow down.

4. Each group member should practice being sensitive to the Spirit and gain confidence in communicating faith and obedience to the Lord.

## 3  Prayer for the Nations

*Ask the Lord how He might have you intercede for a specific city or nation. After responding to the Lord's leading through prophetic actions, make sure to track any changes that appear in the nation by watching the media over the coming days. Often there will be direct correlations to specific things you prayed during these times of prophetic actions and intercession.*

*Here are some simple suggestions to get you started in praying for cities and nations:*

1. Lay hands on a map.

2. Aim your arms in a specific direction.

3. Perform a prayer walk or prayer march.

4. Make movements to a song from that specific nation.

# 4   **Show and Tell**

*In this activation, ask group members to deliver a short prophetic message to one another that includes a prophetic action. This is a great way to practice sharing a message that has a prophetic picture or action associated with it.*

1. For this exercise, you are not allowed to touch the other person or ask the other person to perform any movement or task. The prophetic action or movement will be on the part of the one delivering the word, not the one receiving it. For example, you might stand behind a person with your arms to either side of them like a shield and quote aloud to them Psalm 3:3, "But you are a shield around me, O LORD; you bestow glory on me and lift up my head."

2. The verbal portion of the prophetic word you deliver should be very short and the action non-intrusive.

# Discussion and Reflection Questions

1. Can you think of any other examples of prophetic actions that were performed in Scripture?

   _____

   _____

2. Briefly share any experiences you have had with performing a prophetic action that had a specific outcome or result?

   _____

   _____

3. Why do you think God would want to speak at times through an action rather than a word?

   _____

   _____

4. Below are a few guidelines as criteria for prophetic actions:

   ❖ Prophetic actions should be non-intrusive for the receiver.

   ❖ You should not touch the one who is receiving the word.

   ❖ We do not directly confront spirits of wickedness or darkness over a region through prophetic actions, but rather, we stay focused on the Lord.[27]

---

27  See *Needless Casualties of War* by John Paul Jackson.

5. What would be some other guidelines when using prophetic actions?

_____

_____

6. Which area of prophetic action are you most likely to function in: intercession, communication, or demonstration? Why?

_____

_____

# Notes

Prophecy has become part of our supernatural tool belt for sharing the Good News of Jesus with pre-Christians.

# PROPHETIC EVANGELISM

## CHAPTER NINE

*Objective: Share prophetic encouragement with pre-Christians.*

The first letter to the church at Corinth tells us that prophecy in the church is for encouragement, comfort, and strengthening the body. In the same chapter, however, it speaks of the role of prophecy for the unbeliever.

> *But everyone who prophesies speaks to men for their strengthening, encouragement and comfort* (1 Corinthians 14:3).

> *But if an unbeliever or someone who does not understand comes in while everybody is prophesying, he will be convinced by all that he is a sinner and will be judged by all, and the secrets of his heart will be laid bare. So he will fall down and worship God, exclaiming, "God is really in this place"* (vs. 24-25).

In a world filled with psychics, witches, sorcerers, and movies about magic, our modern culture is demonstrating a greater hunger for supernatural encounters than ever before. The church has a great responsibility to be like Jesus in the demonstration of power and love to the world. Paul determined not to speak with persuasive words but to demonstrate the power and gifts of the Holy Spirit.

> *My message and my preaching were not with wise and persuasive words, but with a demonstration of the Spirit's power, so that your faith might not rest on men's wisdom, but on God's power* (1 Corinthians 2:4).

The primary purpose of prophetic evangelism is to share the Good News of the Kingdom with those who do not yet know Christ. The Good News is not only the message of salvation, but also includes all the benefits of living in His Kingdom. Let's look at a few of those benefits.

> *Praise the LORD, O my soul, and forget not all his benefits—who forgives all your sins and heals all your diseases, who redeems your life from the pit and crowns you with love and compassion, who satisfies your desires with good things so that your youth is renewed like the eagle's* (Psalm 103:2-5).

Jesus sent His disciples out with a message, with power, and with authority.[28] After the day of Pentecost they were also specifically equipped with prophecy.[29] Prophecy has become part of our supernatural tool belt for sharing the Good News of Jesus. We can bring any of the benefits of the Kingdom as a demonstration of the Good News: forgiveness of sins, healing, redemption, love and compassion, satisfied desires, restored youth, deliverance from demons, resurrection, and prophetic encouragement.

---

28  See Matthew 10:8.
29  See Acts 2.

Prophecy is part of the light and good works that draw people to salvation.[30] The importance of this gift in evangelism was emphasized to me twenty-five years ago in a shopping mall in Sweden.

### Ulf

I was a young man teaching in a mission school in Gothenburg, Sweden. At the close of the week-long session the group went to the streets to do some evangelism in a shopping mall. Tired of speaking through an interpreter, I specifically looked for someone who could speak English.

I found my target for blessing in a tall and slender punk rocker named Ulf. Ulf was wrapped in leather from shoulders to toes with a tattered red Ramones T-shirt offering the only contrast to the black leather package. His eyes were dark with eyeliner; ears thick with rings; and a large citrus-colored Mohawk garnished the top of his head. I engaged Ulf in conversation and found him to be a brilliant atheist. Ulf argued against the existence of God, but I had been prepared with apologetic theological studies to defend my faith. A crowd gathered around our spirited debate including several of the students from the school I had taught.

During our conversation I kept having chest pains around the area of my heart. The still small voice within me was saying, "This is a word of knowledge for Ulf." But with the crowd and the students watching, I was too afraid of being wrong or looking foolish, so I continued with my persuasive words. The heart pain continued.

Finally Ulf threw his hands in the air and shouted, "It doesn't matter any way." Ulf's sudden outburst quieted the crowded halls

---

30  See Matthew 5:16.

of the shopping mall.

"What doesn't matter?" I asked gently.

Ulf replied with desperation, "I will find out whether there is a God soon enough. I have an enlarged heart and the doctors have given me only weeks to live."

With that, Ulf suddenly darted away and disappeared into the crowd. His announcement and sudden departure happened so fast that I stood frozen, stunned, and speechless.

Slowly the realization crept in...*if Ulf died without knowing Christ, I was partly responsible.* My fear of failure had kept me from presenting indisputable evidence of the existence of a loving God. The chest pains I was feeling could have spoken directly to Ulf's greatest need, but in those moments, I was more focused with mere arguments and theological debates.

I prayed for Ulf many days after that encounter, but I also determined in my heart that I would never let that happen again. Instead, I would take chances and risks. I would rather be wrong than hold back life-giving information because of fear and pride. I repented to the Lord for my disobedience and devoted myself again to demonstrating God's power and goodness.

I have had many great testimonies of breakthrough over the many years since this incident, but Ulf's story is a haunting remembrance to me that prophetic evangelism is not just a fun little option for blessing. For some, it is a matter of life-or-death.

# Preparing for Prophetic Evangelism

Many of our activations so far have been in a group or classroom setting; perhaps you are even going through this book alone at home. It is time now to take your gifts out into the world. That can be a little frightening at first, but there are many great and rewarding adventures awaiting those who prepare themselves for prophetic evangelism.

Here are a few guidelines to help get you started.

## Be Prepared

*Be prepared in season and out of season...*(2 Timothy 4:2).

*Prepare your minds for action...*(1 Peter 1:13).

*Always be prepared to give an answer to everyone who asks you to give the reason for the hope that you have. But do this with gentleness and respect* (1 Peter 3:15).

The activations we have given you in previous chapters are to prepare you for prophetic encounters. You will find that God will often speak to you with no prophetic trigger whatsoever. Other times we use a method—or trigger—to get us started, and then the prophetic flows in a stronger way.

Preparing yourself is simply exercising an expectation for God-encounters. Prepare your mind by meditating on ways that you can share prophetic encouragement with others.

Read over the activations in the Appendix at the end of this book and think of ways you could use them in everyday life. Let yourself dream and imagine what it looks like to minister to others in this way.

Also, it is good to know how to lead someone in a prayer of salvation. Often I will jot down a few triggers in the morning or send off a prophetic email to get the day started in a supernatural direction.

Prepare yourself for action with expectancy, rehearsal, simple triggers, and obedient action.

## Be Yourself

When giving a prophecy on the streets or at work, it is important to be yourself. Use a normal conversational voice, words, and tone. Be polite and respectful. When approaching a stranger say, "Excuse me." Even if you are rejected or cut off say, "thank you." Don't force a prophetic word on someone. Demonstrate the fruit of the Spirit in love, kindness, gentleness, and patience while presenting the gifts of the Spirit.

> *Always be prepared to give an answer to everyone who asks you to give the reason for the hope that you have. But do this with gentleness and respect* (1 Peter 3:15).

> *Let your conversation be always full of grace, seasoned with salt, so that you may know how to answer everyone* (Colossians 4:6).

## Take the Risk

Risk is another word for faith. You can not wait to activate the prophetic until you have no doubts whatsoever. Have faith by acting on the confidence that God loves people and wants to bless them through you. Take a chance. There will seldom be times when everything is perfect for delivering a word. Courage is not the absence of fear, but rather, the grace to overcome it.

> *And without faith it is impossible to please God, because anyone who comes to him must believe that he exists and that he rewards those who earnestly seek him* (Hebrews 11:6).

*As the body without the spirit is dead, so faith without deeds is dead* (James 2:26).

## The Joyous Call

Evangelism is the joyous call of every believer. Prophetic tools equip us in this mission to have more than fine-sounding philosophies or religious opinions; our prophetic giftings and insights confront the pre-Christian with the reality of God's power and presence. A prophetic word not only reveals the secrets of the heart of the pre-Christian, but also unveils the heart and mind of a loving, heavenly Father who is fully conscious of His lost son or daughter's life and circumstance.

Many people have heard "God so loved the world," but prophecy makes it personal. Prophecy screams, "God loves me! God thinks about *me*. God knows me intimately." The prophetic uncovers the personal love and intimate awareness of God for the individual that compels us to share the Good News with all creation.

To further equip you in this mission of love and power, practice the following prophetic evangelism activations.

# Recommended Prophetic Activations

## 1 No Christianese Please

*This activation is great practice for sharing prophetic words on the streets. With this exercise, practice sharing prophetic words without using our Christian subculture language or jargon that a pre-Christian would not understand.*

1. Have your group suggest phrases that Christians often use but that an unbeliever may not understand.

2. Write these words on a whiteboard, chalkboard or large pad of paper.

3. Now ask two volunteers to come to the front of the room. The first volunteer will prophesy over the other without using any of the Christianese words written on the board. This is harder than you may think.

4. Let several volunteers try prophesying without using Christian jargon. You may want to use a buzzer, bell, or a cell phone tone to warn the person when they have used a word from the forbidden list. (This is like the game Taboo™.)

5. For individual activation, make a photocopy of prophetic words that you have received. Read through the words and highlight any phrases that use Christianese or Christian jargon phrases. Rewrite the phrases using words that a pre-Christian would understand without significantly altering the meaning. In this way you can practice your vocabulary for prophetic evangelism.

## 2 Treasure Hunts

*Kevin Dedmon, one of the pastors at Bethel Church in Redding, California, has made famous the concept of using words of knowledge for evangelistic treasure hunts.[31] Many people have been saved, healed or greatly touched by God's love through this kind of prophetic evangelism.*

1. In a group of three to five people, ask God for words of knowledge that give specifics about people's names, clothing, appearance, and prayer needs. Also, ask God for words of knowledge about locations and other unusual things.

2. Write these clues down on a paper. This is your "treasure map."

3. The team will travel to the location on the map to find these "treasures" of people according to the specific clues received.

4. When the person who fits the clues is found, show this person the treasure map.

5. Ask the person if you can pray for their specific need.

## 3 Personal Treasure Hunt

*Each day can be an adventure in prophetic evangelism. You can do personal treasure hunts on your own to increase the number of divine appointments in your daily routine.*

1. During your morning devotional time, write out several clues of peoples' names, clothing, appearance, and prayer needs that come to mind.

---

31 *The Ultimate Treasure Hunt* by Kevin Dedmon explains this concept fully.

2. Watch and pray for these ministry opportunities to appear during your daily routine at work, school, or around the neighborhod.

## 4  Prophetic Name Badges II

*Here is an exercise based on another skill we learned in Chapter One, "What's in a Name." This activation is designed particularly for teams of people.*

1. Send teams to places where people normally wear name badges, i.e., a restaurant, grocery store, bank, or a local convenience store.

2. At an appropriate time, take a quick moment to share a prophetic word based on the worker's name.

3. If you are sitting in a restaurant, order something to eat. Share your prophetic word with the waiter as the opportunity arises. Make sure to leave a big tip!

4. It is really important to keep your prophetic ministry very brief so as not to keep the employee from his work responsibilities.

# Discussion and Reflection Questions

1. Is there anyone in your daily routine that you would like to target for a prophetic encouragement? How will you prepare yourself to bless them?

   _____

   _____

2. Rate yourself on a boldness scale when it comes to prophetic evangelism with friends, family members, or strangers:

   1 = Always bold, comfortable, and confident.

   2 = Sometimes comfortable or confident.

   3 = Not comfortable or confident.

   A. How can you get more comfortable and confident in sharing prophetic encouragement?

   _____

   _____

   B. What is your greatest obstacle in prophetic evangelism?

   _____

   _____

C. What is your greatest strength when it comes to this ministry?

_____

_____

3. Athletes often visualize themselves winning or achieving specific goals. Do you see visualization and imagination as a valid spiritual tool for building confidence and achieving goals? Why, or, why not?

_____

_____

4. What is your favorite method of prophetic activation and why?

_____

_____

# Notes

God has assigned people spheres of influence where their prophetic gifts and graces have the greatest impact.

# A WORD FOR SEVEN MOUNTAINS

## CHAPTER TEN

*Objective: Explore the idea of influencing the seven mountains of society. Activate prophetically within your primary sphere of influence.*

The Great Commission is a world mandate for all creation.

*He said to them, "Go into all the world and preach the good news to all creation"* (Mark 16:15).

In 1975, Bill Bright, founder of Campus Crusade for Christ, and Loren Cunningham, founder of Youth With A Mission (YWAM), had lunch together. God simultaneously gave each of them a message to give to the other:

*"The culture is shaped by seven mind molders, or mountains, in*

*society. If we can influence each of these areas for Christ, we will win the culture of our nation."*

During that same time frame, Francis Schaeffer was given a similar message.

The seven mountains revealed to these three world influencers are: business, government, media, arts and entertainment, education, the family, and religion.

Many believers have dreams or words about prophesying over world leaders, entertainers, or business moguls. I believe that God wants that to happen. But how will it happen? Perhaps more importantly, how will you prepare yourself for that meeting?

*Have nothing to do with godless myths and old wives' tales; rather, train yourself to be godly. For physical training is of some value, but godliness has value for all things, holding promise for both the present life and the life to come (1 Timothy 4:7-8).*

*Everyone who competes in the games goes into strict training. They do it to get a crown that will not last; but we do it to get a crown that will last forever (1 Corinthians 9:25).*

The purpose of this book and its activations is to help you train yourself for godliness. We learn through knowledge, but we train by exercise.

*Do not merely listen to the word, and so deceive yourselves. Do what it says (James 1:22).*

Faith is like a muscle that must be exercised. No one would enter a national sports competition if they had not trained or competed on that level. Truthfully, they would not even be allowed to compete because they are unqualified for that level of competition. In the same way, many people think that they will influence national leaders, entertainers, or millionaires without any training at all. All things are possible, but that idea is not very probable. God honors faith that has action behind it. The size of your faith is not determined by how much you think you believe, but rather on what level you have exercised that belief.

People often tell me that they have million-dollar faith. "That's great," I reply. "And, to what level is your faith currently exercised?" Usually I just get a dumbfounded look. I truly do not doubt the potential of that person's faith is for millions of dollars. But saying you have faith for a million dollars when you are not seeing provision for small amounts is like saying you believe you will win the 100-meter Olympic hurdles because you sit on the couch watching them on TV. Any person can get in shape. Any person could potentially run faster or lift a heavier weight, but potential doesn't determine performance, training does. Perhaps you could lift two hundred pounds someday, but how much can you lift right now? Your potential may be two hundred pounds, but your performance may be one hundred and twenty. That's okay. Now you know what you must do to train for that level.

Returning to the money metaphor, you have the potential to believe God for millions of dollars, but what level are you currently performing at? Do you commonly give hundreds, or thousands? Have you believed the Lord for large amounts before and seen results? It would be good for most of us to be more honest in evaluating the difference between our potential faith and our current exercise of that faith. The distance between the two determines your need for training.

## What Area Should I Train In?

In a track and field event there are over twenty potential disciplines one could compete in. These events range from running and jumping to throwing to combinations of many disciplines together like the decathlon. An athlete would train differently for each area of focus. Athletes in a throwing event don't need to spend most of their training time running. Those competing in a jumping event don't need to know how to throw.

In the same way it is helpful to know which "events" prophetically you should be training for. Scripture reveals that is was Paul's goal to exercise his gift within the specific sphere of influence that God had given him.

> *But we will not boast beyond our measure, but within the measure of the sphere which God apportioned to us as a measure, to reach even as far as you. For we are not overextending ourselves, as if we did not reach to you, for we were the first to come even as far as you in the gospel of Christ; not boasting beyond our measure, that is, in other men's labors, but with the hope that as your faith grows, we will be, within our sphere, enlarged even more by you, so as to preach the gospel even to the regions beyond you, and not to boast in what has been accomplished in the sphere of another* (2 Corinthians 10:13-16, NASB).

In determining what specific area you should train for prophetically, I believe that your prophetic gift can work anywhere. Believers live in an "anyone, anywhere, anytime" Kingdom. While it is true that your gift can work anywhere, your gift works best somewhere—in a specific geographic or demographic area. This is what Paul was talking about in the above passage as "the measure of the sphere." In modern terms we often call this "your sphere of influence." Just as God has given each of us different gifts, He has also assigned people spheres of influence where their gifts and graces can have the greatest impact.

The easiest way to determine a sphere of influence is when God just "tells" you or assigns you to a specific area. But there are many ways that God "speaks" to us. He can also speak through the realm of observation. If you do not know specifically where God has assigned you, then you might want to ask the following questions:[32]

1. In what area have I seen the greatest amount of influence, favor, and authority?

---

[32] See Prophetic Activation Exercise #15 "Finding Your Mountain of Influence" at the end of this chapter and in the Appendix of Prophetic Activations.

2. In what areas do the task, results, and promotion come most easily to me?

3. Where have I seen the most success with the least amount of effort?

4. In what area am I motivated to work hard and persevere?

5. In what area do people most respond to my gift or input?

Answers to questions like these can help you determine where your greatest sphere of influence might be.

When it comes to prophecy, I have seen many students who were fluent at prophesying over one another in the church. Others in the group seemed to not get much information or clarity. When we took that same group to the streets or the marketplace, however, the roles often reversed. The persons who were fluent and clear in the church suddenly seemed to have less to say, while the quiet ones were now speaking up with clarity and depth.

At first I thought it related to fear levels or comfort levels. Then I came to understand that while our prophetic gift works everywhere, it works best in our specific sphere of influence. The members of the group who performed easily in the church were most likely called to the mountain of religion, while those who had greater grace on the streets were likely called to one of the other seven mountains.

# Recommended Prophetic Activations

**1**    **Finding Your Mountain of Influence**

*With this exercise, determine which of the seven mountains is your strongest sphere of influence by taking time to answer these five questions. The seven mountains are: Family, Religion, Business, Government, Education, Arts and Entertainment, and Media.*

1. In what area have I seen the greatest amount of influence, favor and authority?

   _____

2. In what areas do the task, results, and promotion come most easily to me?

   _____

3. Where have I seen the most success with the least amount of effort?

   _____

4. In what area am I motivated to work hard and persevere in?

   _____

5. In what area do people most positively respond to my gift or input?

   _____

If the questions are difficult for you to answer, pair up with a close friend, family member, or leader who knows you well. Sometimes others can spot our graces and giftings better than we can.

## 2  Prophetic Training Journal

*Once you have determined your primary mountain of influence, you are ready to begin a prophetic training journal.*

*Select a dedicated notebook or journal for this exercise because you will use it for at least one year. This exercise will make a way to train yourself in godliness for the mountain of influence that God has given you.*

1. Prayerfully select an influential prayer target from your mountain of influence. For instance, if your mountain is government, you will probably want to choose a national, state, or local leader as your target. If your mountain is family, you could choose a family in your church, an extended family member, or even the marriage of a public figure or celebrity. If your mountain is education, you could choose a local teacher or national scientist or professor.

2. Once you have chosen your primary prayer target, ask the Lord for specific information regarding your target. Ask Him for Scriptures, prophetic promises, promotions, and/or challenges that your target person will face. Important Note: In this exercise, you will never share these things with the person you are focused on. This activation is still part of your training program. You are training in the secret place for what you believe will happen in the future.

3. Journal all of the clues, proclamations, promises, and prayers that you receive for your target person. In your journal, put a date by all of the prophetic information and activations that you do on your target's behalf. Now pay attention to the news media for reports that validate or confirm the information you were getting from God regarding this person.

4. Keep prophesying, tracking your accuracy, and measuring the

effect of your expressed blessings in the life of your target without ever establishing communication with the person.

5. Once you have built your faith muscle, skill level, clarity and confidence in the secret place, you will be ready to be a strong prophetic source of encouragement in the future.

# 3   Seven Mountain Prophetic Groups

*Once you have identified the primary mountains of influence within your group, gather in small groups that represent the interest of each mountain of society.*

1. Have each group pray for prophetic information regarding their specific mountain of influence.

2. Compare, clarify, and confirm what each group member is hearing by sharing what you are receiving with others.

3. Take time to declare together the prophetic directions that resonate in the strongest way with your group.

# Discussion and Reflection Questions

1. Would you say that your primary mountain of influence was assigned by God or revealed through observation and/or our study questions? If assigned, were the questions confirming your assignment? If revealed through the study questions, did a sense of assignment, destiny, or excitement come with the discovery?

   _____

   _____

2. At what level would you say that your faith is currently exercised for your mountain—beginner, amateur, pro? What examples could you give for why you believe your faith is at that level?

   _____

   _____

3. Reread Paul's statements in 2 Corinthians 10:13-16. What do you think Paul's primary sphere of influence was? What was his hope for expanding that sphere of influence?

   _____

   _____

4. Do you think we always get to operate in the sphere of influence that we want to, or are we sometimes assigned to a different mountain or people group? Read Romans 9:1-3 and Galatians 2:7-9. Do you think Paul got to work in the area of his primary passion?

_____

_____

5. What are some other ways you could train yourself in godliness for your mountain of influence?

_____

_____

# Notes

Our goal in a geographic
region is to displace darkness by
displaying light.

# PROPHESYING OVER CITIES, REGIONS, AND NATIONS

## CHAPTER ELEVEN

*Objective: Explore creative ways to prophesy blessing over cities, regions, and nations.*

We not only have permission and authority to interact prophetically with individuals but also with cities, regions, and nations. Old Testament prophets would often speak the word of the Lord over cities, regions, and nations. This type of prophecy was called the "oracle of the Lord." There are at least fourteen examples of this in the books of the prophets.[33]

Jesus prophesied over cities during His physical earthly ministry.

*O Jerusalem, Jerusalem, you who kill the prophets and stone those sent to you, how often I have longed to gather your children together, as a hen gathers her chicks under her wings, but you were not willing. Look, your house is left to you desolate.*

---

33  See Isaiah 13:1, 15:1, 17:1, 19:1, 21:1, 21:11, 21:13, 22:1, 23:1, 30:6; Nahum 1:1; Zechariah 9:1, 12:1; Malachi 1:1.

*For I tell you, you will not see me again until you say, "Blessed is he who comes in the name of the Lord"* (Matthew 23:37-39).

Then Jesus began to denounce the cities in which most of His miracles had been performed because they did not repent.

*Woe to you, Korazin! Woe to you, Bethsaida! If the miracles that were performed in you had been performed in Tyre and Sidon, they would have repented long ago in sackcloth and ashes. But I tell you, it will be more bearable for Tyre and Sidon on the day of judgment than for you. And you, Capernaum, will you be lifted up to the skies? No, you will go down to the depths. If the miracles that were performed in you had been performed in Sodom, it would have remained to this day. But I tell you that it will be more bearable for Sodom on the day of judgment than for you"* (Matthew 11:21-24).

Notice that these negative prophecies were uttered before the sacrifice for sin through the person of Jesus Christ. Because Christ has now taken the judgment and penalty for sin on the cross, we can now announce blessing and destiny over nations. Post-resurrection prophecies over nations and cities should generally follow the same guidelines as stated in 1 Corinthians 14:3, "...for strengthening, encouragement, and comfort."

In addition to prophetic declarations, we are commanded to pray and intercede for nations and their leaders in both the Old and New Testaments.

*Ask of me, and I will make the nations your inheritance and the ends of the earth your possession* (Psalm 2:8).

*I urge, then, first of all, that requests, prayers, intercession and thanksgiving be made for everyone—for kings and all those in authority, that we may live peaceful and quiet lives in all godliness and holiness. This is good, and pleases God our Savior, who wants all men to be saved and to come to a knowledge of the truth* (1 Timothy 2:1-3).

This type of prayer and intercession will often include various forms of prophetic activation like the ones you have studied in earlier chapters. Read through the following examples to see how the activations that you have already studied were used biblically for prophesying over geographical regions. Remember that most Old Testament examples include some sort of judgment for sin because the price had not yet been paid on the cross to make men righteous before God.

Today we would use these same methods to bless cities and proclaim regional and national identity and destiny.

## Names

The prophet Hosea delivers a message for the region of Ephraim based upon the meaning of its name. Ephraim means "fruitful," but they had become blighted, withered, and without fruit. The prophecy is an obvious play on words using the name Ephraim.

> *Ephraim is blighted, their root is withered, they yield no fruit...* (Hosea 9:16).

### Vacaville

The city that I live in is called Vacaville. It's a beautiful suburban community at the foot of a small mountain range. In Spanish, the name Vacaville is similar to the words for "cow" and "town." For this reason many people refer to us as "cow-town." (Our city was actually named in the mid-1800's after one of its most influential families, the Vaca family.) There are no cows within the city limits of the town, but cattle do sometimes graze on the foothills of a greenbelt just west of the city.

I like to use the name trigger to prophesy over my city. In Psalm 50:11, God speaks of His prosperity as being like the cattle on a

167

thousand hills. Prophetically, we see our city name and the cows on the hills as a declaration of a place of God's prosperity and provision.

## Objects

Jeremiah saw a boiling pot tilting away from the north. The pot represented an attack from foreign kings upon the nation of Israel.

*The word of the LORD came to me again: "What do you see?"*

*"I see a boiling pot, tilting away from the north," I answered. The LORD said to me, "From the north disaster will be poured out on all who live in the land. I am about to summon all the peoples of the northern kingdoms," declares the LORD. "Their kings will come set up their thrones in the entrance of the gates of Jerusalem..."* (Jeremiah 1:13-15).

Jeremiah's prophetic training using objects was always in preparation for prophesying over cities, regions, and nations. Today, many nations have a national symbol. The United States' symbol is an eagle. These symbols are really just prophetic pictures focused around a specific virtue or special feature of the nation. In the same way, God can speak through objects and symbols to release new virtues, identities, and blessings over a specific geographical region.

## Writing

Daniel and the party at Babylon literally saw a hand write words on the wall of the palace. The words were a prophetic message to the leader of the nation.

*Therefore he sent the hand that wrote the inscription. "This is the inscription that was written: Mene, Mene, Tekel, Parsin. "This is what these words mean: Mene: God has numbered the days of your reign and brought it to an end. Tekel: You have been weighed in the scales and found wanting. Peres: Your kingdom is divided and given to the Medes and Persians* (Daniel 5:24-28).

It is not difficult to see the connection between creative writing and the ability to influence cities, regions, and nations. Think of how writings like Upton Sinclair's *The Jungle* or Harriet Beecher Stowe's *Uncle Tom's Cabin* have shaped the thoughts and structure of America. Other nations have been transformed through strategic writings also. Consider how Karl Marx's *The Communist Manifesto* impacted world governments and international relations in the 20th century. Likewise, prophetic stories like *Piercing the Darkness*[34] and *The Shack*[35] have sold millions of copies in modern America and transformed how many people see God and the spiritual world. Of course, the most transformational prophetic writing of all times is the Bible.

## Prophetic Song

Jennifer grew up in a small island paradise deep in the South Pacific. One day, while in prayer for the nation, God gave the young blonde girl a prophetic song for the nation. Though I do not remember the exact details, I know that Jennifer's family had a great reputation as missionaries and were a positive influence of the culture. As a result, Jennifer was able to share her song with the president of the nation.

Reportedly, he was so moved by the song, that he had her prophetic song sung along with the national anthem at public gatherings during his tenure as president.

---

34    by Frank Peretti.
35    by William P. Young.

## Senses

In Chapter Four we learned how to train our senses for personal prophetic ministry. Our senses can also be exercised on a local, regional, or global level to get insights over cities, regions, and nations. Cities will often have actual natural smells that speak of their agricultural or industrial specialties. These same smells may speak of some prophetic destiny.

Consider what your city may smell like in the Spirit. What are symbols, landmarks, or specific geographic features that may give prophetic insights into your city or region?

Your city can also have a feel—it may not be specifically tactile, but many cities will give off a feeling or vibe. Could this sensation also be prophetic? I believe it is.

Practice using each of your five senses, both naturally and spiritually, to gain prophetic insight into your city, region, and nation. God is using these gateways of perception to increase our sensitivity to His heart and thoughts over specific geographic regions.

## Actions

In Chapter Eight we saw how God used prophetic actions and His foreknowledge to speak to cities, regions, and nations. Below is a testimony of such an action.

### Planting a Small Seed

One of the great generals of intercession shares the story of how an intercessory team he led performed a prophetic act of planting a spiritual seed in the ground of the main square of a communist country. I imagine that even this experienced group of radical intercessors felt a little self-conscious as they lifted an invisible seed up to Heaven and then acted as if they were planting it in the ground and covering it over with dirt.

Years later, the spot where they prophetically planted this seed was the exact site of the cultural revolution that overthrew the country and brought spiritual, social, and financial freedom to the nation.

Simple prophetic acts directed by the Spirit can impact cities, regions, and nations, and I have heard so many great testimonies through the years. I have also heard a few horror stories.

There are a few things to consider when performing a prophetic act over a geographical region. First, remember that you are engaging in something bigger than yourself that impacts many people. You may be acting on land that is not your own. Therefore, it is often both wise and helpful to have other people, landowners, or leaders judge and be involved in any prophetic act that will potentially impact a city, region, or nation. This precaution will help you know you are not acting independently beyond your own God-given authority or assigned sphere of influence.

Remember from Chapter Eight that we do not recommend directly confronting spiritual powers of darkness or wicked authority through a prophetic action. Rather, our goal is to displace darkness by displaying light. Our focus is always on the King and His Kingdom. As instructed in Jude,[36] we are careful not to "slander celestial beings," principalities, or authorities with a prophetic action or declaration. We do not confront anything with fear, but we do engage it with wisdom. In their zeal, the Sons of Thunder wanted to call down fire on cities, but Jesus cautioned them to know what spirit they were operating in.[37]

Finally, let us remember that the nature of the New Testament prophecy

---

36   Jude 8-9.
37   See Luke 9:54-55.

is to bless and build up. Any prophetic action should be consistent with this standard. Our primary mandate is to release blessings over cities, regions, and nations, not to pronounce curses or judgments. Even Jesus did not come "to condemn the world, but to save the world"[38] through Himself.

Because prophetic actions are such a powerful tool and can affect many lands and people, we are careful to perform prophetic acts over cities, regions, and nations in the right spirit, and with the counsel and blessing of local and national leaders.

God has called believers to disciple nations and impact cities. He has also given us the tools to do it. Let's partner together with others within the Body of Christ to see specific geographic regions transformed for the glory of God.

Now, let us apply all that we have learned about using names, vision, writing, our senses, and prophetic actions with specific activations as they relate to the sphere of cities, regions, nations.

---

38   John 3:17.

# Recommended Prophetic Activations

## 1 Blessing Your City

*Take time to meditate on what the Lord is saying to bless your city.*

1. Write down your ideas on a piece of paper.

2. Gather as a group and declare them over your city as if it were a person standing in front of you.

3. You may want to speak these prophetic words at a strategic location within your city, i.e., at the highest point of the city, the entrance to the city, or at the governmental center, etc.

4. Take turns speaking prophetic blessings over your city and then write them down so that you can watch them come to pass in the days ahead.

## 2 Blessing National Leaders

*This exercise provides intentional opportunities to bless the political leaders of your nation.*

1. Make a list of strategic national leaders.

2. Print pictures of them if you can and have them in front of you.

3. Pray and ask the Lord for prophetic words of encouragement over your nation's leaders. Write down these prophetic words.

4. If this is a group or public gathering, play some patriotic music over the sound system or through a portable music device. Allow people to make their prophetic declarations over leaders you are

targeting. Speak as if those leaders are actually standing right in front of you.

5. Create crafted prayers around the prophetic words and pray them often, declaring the blessings of the Lord over the political leaders of your nation.

## 3 Prophetic Geographic Collage

*This collage poster makes another great prayer tool to remind you to partner with what God is speaking over specific geographical regions.*

1. Gather stacks of old magazines that you can cut up for this project.

2. Have your group scan through the various advertisements and pictures in the magazines looking for words and images that God is speaking over a specific geographic area, i.e., a city, your region, or a nation.

3. Paste the words and images onto a poster board to make a visual statement of what God is speaking about that geographical region.

## 4 The Sounds of the Nations

*This is a great activation to pray over specific regions or nations.*

1. Collect ethnic music off the internet from various nations where you have mission interests.[39]

---

39  See our Sounds of the Nations recordings on iTunes.

2. Play a single song from each nation and ask friends in your group to craft a prophetic word, picture, image, or sense of what the Lord is speaking over that nation.

3. Move from song to song until all the nations you are focusing on have been covered.

4. After the song time, have everyone stand and declare prophetic words over the nations.

## 5  National Treasure Hunt

*Have a detailed world atlas and Wi-Fi access available for this exercise.*

1. Have group members ask the Lord for the name of a city, region, or nation. Ask God what the prayer needs are in that location. Write down your clues.

2. Research to find where the location is and how the clues you received might match any news events posted on the internet.

3. Pray and declare the clues you have gathered over that place.

## 6  Set a Date

*The truth is, with our busy lives, we often do not remember to pray for our own city, region, or nation. If we don't set an occasion for prayer, then we tend to only pray occasionally. Create an action plan for when you will pray, give thanks and prophesy over your city, region, or nation. I used to call mine "Around the World Wednesdays." On Wednesday mornings I would gather with some friends, and we would pray over and speak to the nations that were upon our hearts.*

1. I recommend that you set a daily, weekly, or monthly appointment for this exercise.

2. Journal what and when you prayed and prophesied so that you can track the accuracy and fulfillments.

## 7 Prayer for the Nations

*Ask the Lord how He might have you intercede for a specific city or nation. After responding to the Lord's leading through prophetic actions, make sure to track any changes that appear in the nation by watching the media over the coming days. Often there will be direct correlations to specific things you prayed during these times of prophetic actions and intercession.*

*Here are some simple suggestions to get you started in praying for cities and nations:*

1. Lay hands on a map.

2. Aim your arms in a specific direction.

3. Perform a prayer walk or prayer march.

4. Make movements to a song from that specific nation.

# Discussion and Reflection Questions

1. What geographical region stirs the greatest passion in you—local, regional, or global? From what you have learned in this chapter, how will you interact prophetically with your primary geographic passion?

   _____

   _____

2. How often do you currently pray for or prophesy over governmental leaders? Reread the passage in 1 Timothy 2:1-3. What would you say is the priority level placed upon praying for leaders in this Scripture? Can you think of examples of prophets who prayed and prophesied over national leaders? How closely does your priority match that of Scripture?

   _____

   _____

3. What is your city or region best known for? What prophetic actions might be a blessing or carry influence within your own city? Brainstorm with a group and then build a potential action plan for carrying out some of your ideas. Remember that we do not focus on the problems or spirits of darkness in our city, but rather on the answers, blessings, and the light.

   _____

_____

_____

_____

_____

4. How do you stay globally aware? What is your main source of information? How accurate do you feel the information is that you are receiving? What other ways might you increase your global awareness?

_____

_____

_____

_____

# Notes

Process your prophetic
words and put them into
active service.

# PROPHETIC PROCESSING

## CHAPTER TWELVE

*Objective: Judge, process, and mobilize prophetic words that you have received.*

Prophecy is not just about giving words, but also about what we do with the words we have been given. In past times, I thought the best thing you could do with a prophecy is to put it on the "back burner" and wait to see if it comes true. Now, I believe that we must first judge a prophetic word to see if we believe it is an accurate representation of what the Lord is saying.

> *Do not put out the Spirit's fire; do not treat prophecies with contempt. Test everything. Hold on to the good* (1 Thessalonians 5:19-21).

*Two or three prophets should speak, and the others should weigh carefully what is said* (1 Corinthians 14:29).

# Judging a Prophetic Word

Some of the ways we can judge a word is through the following criteria.

* Does it agree with Scripture?

* Is it consistent with the character and nature of God?

* Does it resonate with me? Do I feel the word is true even if parts of it challenge me? Is the word taking me in a direction that is counter to my will or sense of peace?

* How do family, friends, and leaders who love me feel about the word?

* Do I trust the source? Does the person giving the word have any reason to control or manipulate me? Would the person delivering the word receive any personal benefit from my following this prophetic word?

* Does it glorify God and draw me closer to Jesus?

* Based upon these criteria, do I and those who love me believe this word or parts of it accurately reflect what God is speaking to me right now?

Notice from the above letter to the Corinthians that judging a word is a group exercise. We should involve others in the processing of our prophetic words, and yet we must personally take responsibility for the final decision.

Returning to 1 Thessalonians 5:19-21, we have a command to not treat prophecies with contempt, but rather to test all of it and hold on to the parts that are good. That means some parts of a prophecy can be accurate while other parts may be discarded. That is because prophecy comes as partial information.

*For we know in part, and we prophesy in part* (1 Corinthians 13:9).

As we said in the Introduction, getting a prophetic word (or part of a prophetic word) wrong does not make you a false prophet. False prophets are those who have an ulterior motive for delivering the word. False prophets can even have the correct word but be wrong in their motive or reason for giving the word. Balaam's prophetic words were accurate, but he was prophesying for personal gain and profit.[40]

Scripture places the heaviest responsibility on the one judging the word rather than the one delivering the word. Of course we want to be accurate, but we will never step out if we are afraid of making a mistake and being labeled a false prophet.

We must all take responsibility to test the spirits and to judge the prophetic words that we have received.

*Dear friends, do not believe every spirit, but test the spirits to see whether they are from God, because many false prophets have gone out into the world* (1 John 4:1).

## Processing a Prophetic Word

Once we have judged a word to be an accurate representation of what God is speaking, then it is time to dig more fully into the word. We call this prophetic processing. Paul told his spiritual son, Timothy, to "fight the good fight" by following the prophecies that had been made about him.

*Timothy, my son, I give you this instruction in keeping with the prophecies once made about you, so that by following them you may fight the good fight* (1 Timothy 1:18).

---

40  See 2 Peter 2:15 and Jude 11.

Paul's instruction to his spiritual son does not sound like putting the word on the back burner to wait and see if it comes true. This spiritual giant commanded his student to follow the prophetic words and to fight with them. The word "fight" here is the Greek word *strateuo.* It means "to enlist in a military expedition, to lead soldiers into a battle; to put into active service."

Here are a few of the ways you can begin to process your prophetic words[41] to put them into active service:

- ❖ Type out and double-space the prophetic words that you want to process.

- ❖ Circle any words that refer to who God says you are. We call these "identity words."

- ❖ Underline any promises that God is making directly to you.

- ❖ Make note of any conditions or requirements on your part.

- ❖ Mark any words that indicate timing or seasons.

- ❖ Make a list of any metaphors or biblical references that you want to research further.

- ❖ Notice how many times a word, idea, or theme is repeated. Determine major and minor themes within your prophetic words.

The goal of prophetic processing is to gain a clear and accurate view of what it is God is speaking to you through your prophetic words.

## Mobilizing a Prophetic Word

When a person has judged his prophetic words to be accurate and has processed them to clearly understand what God is speaking, he then has the power to put them into action.

---

41   See "Processing A Prophetic Word Worksheet" in the Appendix of Prophetic Activation Worksheets.

Jesus mobilized the words that God had spoken over Him to fight off the tempter.

> *The tempter came to him and said, "If you are the Son of God, tell these stones to become bread." Jesus answered, "It is written: Man does not live on bread alone, but on every word that comes from the mouth of God"* (Matthew 4:3-4).

How does this passage speak of mobilizing a prophetic word? Remember what had just happened to Jesus a few verses before? Jesus had just been baptized by John in the Jordan River, and the heavens opened up. The Holy Spirit descended upon Jesus and a voice came from heaven declaring His prophetic calling.

> *And a voice from heaven said, "This is my Son, whom I love; with him I am well pleased"* (Matthew 3:17).

One reason that Jesus could not be tempted to perform for the devil is because He so clearly knew who the Father said He was. When Jesus quoted to the tempter that man was to live by the words that come from the mouth of God, He was referring to the words God had just spoken over Him. God had already declared that Jesus was His Son, that He loved Him, and was completely pleased with Him. By knowing what the Father had said to Him, Jesus could not be tempted to prove it through activity that the Father had not required or desired.

Mobilizing prophetic words can begin with these four simple steps:

1. Ask God what He is saying to you.

2. Agree with what God is saying through processing, studying, and meditating on it.

3. Align yourself in character and behavior with what God is saying.

4. Appropriate your mindset, time, and resources towards the direction

that is consistent with what God is saying about you. Take appropriate actions.

Mobilizing prophetic words is not just about acting out your promises, it is also about living and acting as the person Heaven says you are. Prophetic mobilization is warring with your prophetic words until your circumstances bow to the promises of God. Processing and mobilization helps us to know what to do in the gap between the promise and the fulfillment. Our character, resources, and mindsets come into alignment with the promises of God, so that as prophetic blessings are realized, they are also sustained.

Learning to process and mobilize your prophetic words is perhaps the most important activation of all.

# Recommended Prophetic Activations

## 1 Prophetic Identity Statement

*A prophetic identity statement is a written declaration of who God says you are based on the words and phrases He uses to describe you within your personal prophecies. This exercise will be useful for other activations. Use the "Prophetic Identity Statement Worksheet" in the Appendix of Prophetic Activation Worksheets to complete this activation.*

1. Using the circled words from your prophetic processing exercise,[42] make a list of the descriptive phrases embedded in your prophetic words that speak to your identity.

2. From this list of phrases, compose a short biographical paragraph of three to five sentences that describe who God says that you are. Start your paragraph with the statement, "I am..."

3. Once everyone has composed their prophetic identity statements, have them read the statements before the rest of the group.

4. Practice relating to one another according to the way God describes each person. Hold one another accountable to living as the people God says you are.

5. For individual activation, determine to align your character, thoughts, and behavior with the truth of who God says you are. What changes in thought patterns or behaviors will you need to make? Rehearse your prophetic identity statement until you have memorized it and it becomes imbedded in your spirit.

---

42   See "Processing a Prophetic Word" in Chapter 12 and  use the "Processing a Prophetic Word Worksheet" in the Appendix of Prophetic Activation Worksheets.

## 2  Crafted Prayer

*A crafted prayer can be formulated from key elements of a promise from God or a prophetic word that was received—for yourself or for someone else.*

1. Take key statements of promise from the Lord that are embedded in your prophetic words and craft them into a prayer. For example, you might begin your crafted prayer with, "Lord, You said that You would..."

2. Then match each promise with a thanksgiving, a declaration of intent or identity, and a petition.

## 3  Prophetic Collage of Family Crest

*For this exercise, gather stacks of old magazines that can be cut up. Use your prophetic identity statement to create a prophetic collage or family crest.*

1. Cut out pictures and words that relate directly to your prophetic identity[43] and paste them into a collage.

2. For a family crest, you may want to choose the 3-4 dominant thoughts from your prophetic identity statement and find an image that represents each one.

3. Paste these images onto a shield or crest shape along with a strategic phrase or two.

---

43    See "Prophetic Identity Statement Worksheet" in the Appendix of Prophetic Activation Worksheets.

# 4   MAP (Ministry Action Plan)

*You can create a MAP for each of the major promises the Lord has given you with this exercise.*

1. List one of the primary promises God has made concerning you.

2. Under that promise, list the potential areas you will need to develop in order to embrace or sustain that level of promise. Consider areas of personal and character development, resource and financial development, strategic partnership and team development, skills development and spiritual development.

3. Write short goals or targets for each area of development that become the MAP to your promise.

# Discussion and Reflection Questions

1. How many prophetic words do you have over your life? How many of them seem significant to you? What has been your level of follow-up with the prophetic words you already have?

   _____

   _____

2. What criteria does your church use for processing prophetic words? How well does your community know your church protocol and prophetic processing criteria? How often have you acted on or mobilized a prophetic word or promise?

   _____

   _____

   _____

   _____

3. Read 2 Corinthians 5:16-17. How does this passage relate to the issue of prophetic identity and how we view one another? What would it look like if accountability were built around our prophetic identity rather than our earthly weaknesses?

   _____

   _____

4. Have you ever received a "bad" prophetic word? What made it bad? What did you do with that word? How did you respond to the one who gave it? What systems of accountability does your church have in place for those who minister in the prophetic?

_____

_____

5. How does a prophetic word compare to the written Word (the Bible) in authority? Does that change once a prophetic word has been judged to be accurate and "from God?" What place of authority should prophetic words have in the life of the believer? How does the Scripture in 1 Timothy 1:18 tie in to your answer?

_____

_____

# Notes

_____

_____

_____

_____

_____

Prophecy is recognizing
God speaking and revealing
Himself so that we may
respond to it.

# CONCLUSION

Now that you have seen and experienced many different ways to activate prophetic grace, you must choose to walk in them. Many Christians wait for powerful things to happen in their lives but never pursue them because of their theological perspective. Most people live as sovereigntists when it comes to the supernatural—believing it is God's responsibility alone to trigger a supernatural event. Obviously you have discovered in this book that I do not adhere to that belief system.

I truly believe that through our divine union with Christ, every son and daughter of God is living in a paradox of what I like to call "the mystery of incarnation." Jesus Christ was not half man and half God; He was fully man and fully God. This is the mystery of the incarnation of Christ, that He could be fully God and fully man at the same time. Though redeemed man is not a god, nor equal to God, he does share, in some ways, Christ's mystery of incarnation.

God is sovereign and can work independently in the lives of individuals without any requirement of a human catalyst or permission. Man has also been graced with the faculty of choice. It is man's responsibility not only to respond to God's sovereign advances, but also to pursue God and take responsibility for the stewardship of his own life and destiny. In this way we are sharing in the mystery of Christ's incarnation—God is fully sovereign and we are completely responsible.

I believe this describes the true relationship of the supernatural lifestyle. The supernatural is as simple as God's super and your natural. God's super speaks of His sovereignty, while the natural speaks of man's responsibility. It is not some or half of each; it is totally and completely both.

Dangers potentially wait on either side of this paradox. The one who leans too heavily on sovereignty waits always for God to initiate. Whenever God initiates through partnership, the opportunity is not recognized, and so it appears that nothing is happening. The outcome is often that very little of the supernatural occurs and the world loses much of the true light of the Kingdom of God. On the other extreme, we find the person who turns these prophetic activations into a mere formula. In the introduction we cautioned: "Prophecy should never be a form or formula. The prophetic is meant to be a divine dialogue with the Holy Spirit. Each of the activations in this book are designed to be a trigger for greater conversation with God." The goal of prophetic grace is to fully embrace this mystery of incarnation. Be led of God, but boldly step out in the gifts, grace, and faith God has given you. I like the way Romans chapter twelve states it.

> *We have different gifts, according to the grace given us. If a man's gift is prophesying, let him use it in proportion to his faith* (Romans 12:6).

God gives us the gifts and the grace. Notice the statements of human responsibility. "Let him use it..." and "...in proportion to his faith." Will you use the gift and the grace that God has given you? Will you activate it and stir up your gift through faith?

My hope in writing *Basic Training for Prophetic Activation* is that while you are learning how to activate prophetic grace upon your life, you also recognize many of the ways that God is already speaking to you. Most of us have been like the boy Samuel in that God has been speaking to us, but we did not recognize it as His voice. Prophecy is really just about recognizing how God is speaking and revealing Himself so that we may respond to it. God desires a divine partnership in releasing His purposes in the earth.

*See, the former things have taken place, and new things I declare; before they spring into being I announce them to you* (Isaiah 42:9).

*However, as it is written: "No eye has seen, no ear has heard, no mind has conceived what God has prepared for those who love him"—but God has revealed it to us by his Spirit"* (1 Corinthians 2:9-10).

I believe that God is looking for divine partnerships to release new things in the earth. The Spirit is training us to recognize His voice so that He can announce these new things to us before they spring forth in the earth. God wants to reveal things that no eye has seen, no ear has heard, and no mind has ever conceived. Previously unimaginable things will be revealed to us by the Spirit of God. That is why divine partnership is so important. We are not just learning to prophesy; we are learning to hear. Hearing God, seeing God, and perceiving His heart through prophetic activation is what makes new things possible in the earth.

So, give your faith some exercise. Take your prophetic grace out for a test drive. Choose to activate your gifts and graces daily like an athlete working his muscles in a gym, training for greatness. Constantly dialogue with Holy Spirit while you are stirring your own gifts, graces, and faith. Take time to enjoy your increased partnership with God. Celebrate your breakthroughs, and learn quickly from your mistakes. Invest yourself in your spiritual development and an increased sense of intimacy with Holy Spirit.

Though this book is coming to its conclusion, your prophetic activation journey has just begun. Continue to recognize new and different ways that God is speaking to and through you. Remain humble and teachable. Stay on track by submitting all prophetic words to judging and processing with others who care for you and the health of the Body of Christ. Review and practice the activations in the Appendix often to keep toning your spiritual muscle and activating your prophetic grace. Watch and listen for new activations and trainings that the Holy Spirit will unveil to you. Share these ideas and activations with others so that everyone might be encouraged, built up, and comforted with the goodness of God.

# Notes

Hearing God, seeing God,
and perceiving His heart through
prophetic activation is what makes
new things possible
in the earth.

# Appendix of Prophetic Activations

Below are the activation exercises recommended in the preceding chapters of this book arranged alphabetically and numbered for quick reference.

I recommend that you review the "Prophetic Protocol for Activations" from the Introduction.

In summary:

❖ Be positive.

❖ Be brief.

❖ Be kind.

❖ Be humble.

## 1 Assigned Identities

*If God renamed you, what new name would He give you?*

1. In a group setting, pair up and have each group member assign a new identity to his partner by changing his name.

2. Prophesy over your partner about why you would give that particular name and describe its prophetic significance.

3. For individual activation, ask the Lord for a new name, or choose one, and then research the meaning. Write all of your research and revelation down in the form of a prophetic word for yourself.

# 2 Appearance Triggers

*For this exercise remember not to judge by appearances, but rather, allow the Lord to draw your attention to a specific detail that triggers a word of prophetic encouragement. Consider that colors, shapes, letters, and numbers can all be a part of triggering the prophetic flow.*

1.  Get with a friend or a small group and practice prophetic encouragement triggered by an item of clothing, jewelry, shoes, words that appear on clothing, or even tattoos.

2.  For individual activation, flip through magazines looking for external triggers for the prophetic through what people are wearing.

# 3 Atmospheric Gift

*Ask God to show you a gift that would be meaningful to the one receiving it. Try to choose a gift with no obvious spiritual meaning. Choose something that the person would see every day, such as a picture, a sculpture, a piece of jewelry, or favorite clothing item. It should be a gift that they would put in a prominent place somewhere in their house. Make sure the gift you purchase is something that the person would really enjoy.*

1.  Write out the name of a family member, friend, or co-worker who does not yet know the Lord.

2.  Purchase the item and take it to your prayer closet. Lay your hands on the item and pray over it often. Soak it with presence while you worship and commune with the Lord. Ask the Lord to anoint

the item like He did the handkerchiefs and aprons that Paul had touched.[44]

3. When you give the gift to this designated person, don't say anything about your spiritual preparation time over it or its prophetic meaning. Just share the gift in the spirit of love and watch to see what happens.

# 4 Back-to-Back

*This exercise works really well in a larger group. Continue alternating groups until each one has delivered back-to-back prophecies over at least three different people.*

1. Have half of your group stand in a line with their backs facing the rest of the group.

2. Now ask the other half of the group to choose one person in the line to stand behind. Stand facing the back of the person you have chosen.

3. When the group leader gives the signal, the first group will turn around and face the person standing behind them. The person who turned around will have only 60 seconds to deliver a word of prophetic encouragement.

4. Next have the second group turn their backs to the first group. Everyone in the first group switches places and stands facing the back of the person they have chosen.

---

44 Acts 19:12.

5. On the signal, the second group will turn and face the members of the first group in their new positions and deliver a 60-second prophetic word.

# 5 Blessing National Leaders

*This exercise provides intentional opportunities to bless the political leaders of your nation.*

1. Make a list of strategic national leaders.

2. Print pictures of them if you can and have them in front of you.

3. Pray and ask the Lord for prophetic words of encouragement over your nation's leaders. Write down these prophetic words.

4. If this is a group or public gathering, play some patriotic music over the sound system or through a portable music device. Allow people to make their prophetic declarations over leaders you are targeting. Speak as if those leaders are standing right in front of you.

5. Create crafted prayers around the prophetic words and pray them often, declaring the blessings of the Lord over the political leaders of your nation.

# 6 Blessing Your City

*Take time to meditate on what the Lord is saying to bless your city.*

1.  Write down your ideas on a piece of paper.

2.  Gather as a group and declare them over your city as if it were a person standing in front of you.

3.  You may want to speak these prophetic words at a strategic location within your city, i.e., at the highest point of the city, the entrance to the city, or at the governmental center, etc.

4.  Take turns speaking prophetic blessings over your city and then write them down so that you can watch them come to pass in the days ahead.

## 7 Blind Phone Book Find

*If this is for a group, collect as many local phone books as you can. Get in small groups of three to five and provide a phone book for each group.*

1.  Have one group member fan through the phone book pages while the member to the right has his eyes closed.

2.  The member with his eyes closed places a finger on a random name in the phone book. Read the name aloud and give a prophetic word for that person using one of the name methods.

3.  Then pass the phone book to the left and continue until everyone in the group has had at least one turn.

4.  While doing this exercise, you may feel strongly about the prophetic word you have given. If so, call the person and actually deliver this word of encouragement to them. You could say something

like, "You don't know me, but I saw your name in the phone book and feel like God wants to share something with you. Would you like to hear it?" If they decline then let them go; if they say "yes," then share the word the Lord leads you to say. Note: Because this is a stranger you are talking to, do not give out any personal information or contact details over the phone. If they ask for contact information, give your local church name, phone number, address, etc.

5. You can perform the same activation on your own. Put the phone book in front of you. Close your eyes and flip quickly through the pages. Without looking, plop your finger down on a name and practice prophesying over the name that is closest to where your finger points.

# 8 Crafted Prayer

*A crafted prayer can be formulated from key elements of a promise from God or a prophetic word that was received—for yourself or for someone else.*

1. Take key statements of promise from the Lord that are embedded in your prophetic words and craft them into a prayer. For example, you might begin your crafted prayer with, "Lord, You said that You would…"

2. Then match each promise with a thanksgiving, a declaration of intent or identity, and a petition.

# 9 Creative Prophetic Writing

*The idea of this exercise is to prepare a prophetic word that is embedded in some form of creative writing. This type of written prophecy works great to share with pre-Christians or those who might not otherwise be open to prophetic ministry.*

1. Prepare a short story, a poem, a song, or devotional thought in written form.

2. This activation is a "carry-out" exercise. People will carry the word with them to work, school, or their neighborhood, watching for opportunities to share it with the right person.

3. Usually the person the creative prophetic writing piece was intended for is someone you already know. If this is the case, you can simply open a conversation with that person by saying, "I wrote a little something (i.e., story, poem, song, inspirational thought) the other day and wondered if you would like to read it?" If it seems appropriate, you can follow up by saying, "I felt like God had me write that specifically for you."

Many times this will make a real connection with the person or open up the opportunity for a deeper conversation on spiritual matters.

# 10 Environmental Triggers

*This activation is a good opportunity to become more aware of our external environment, recognizing that God will use these as clues to give a prophetic encouraging word to someone.*

1. Pair up with a friend or gather a small group.

2. Look around the room and observe your surroundings for something that might immediately attract your attention. Perhaps it is the "exit" sign or a big comfy chair, or maybe you are drawn to a bookshelf, a podium, chalkboard, or an eraser.

3. Take turns in your small group sharing about the item that triggered your attention and what you felt the Lord was speaking through that item.

4. For individual activation, journal the things that God is speaking to you through your external environment.

 11 **Family Ties**

*This is a great way to practice receiving words of knowledge.*

1. Divide your group into pairs. Have them sit in chairs facing one another. It is best to pair up with someone whom you do not know very well.

2. Ask the Lord to give you information about a person in your partner's family. You might see a name, a face, a hair color, a city, a specific situation or need. Share the information with your partner and get feedback on its accuracy. If you appear to miss it, try again with different information. You can rotate pairs two or three times to exercise your "faith muscle" for a word of knowledge.

3. For individual activation, choose three friends, classmates or co-workers. Ask the Lord for the same types of family information and needs. Write down and date the information you receive. Contact

the persons, or wait for an appropriate time to begin a conversation about the person's family. You could say something like, "I was praying for you the other day and wrote these things down about a family member of yours." Show them the paper and offer to pray for them and their family.

## 12 Favorite Bible Character

*Ask the members of your group to choose a favorite Bible character—the one they most admire in character and actions.*

1. Have each one in the group go person-to-person, introducing themselves by the name of their favorite Bible character.

2. Each person will prophesy over the other from a quality that relates to that specific Bible character.

3. For individual activation, ask God for prophetic insights on why you relate to this Bible character. Write the results as a prophetic word in your journal.

## 13 Favorite Fragrance

*You may want to study biblical and extra-biblical sources to understand the greater meanings or specific ingredients of a particular fragrance. By studying something further in the natural realm, we often will increase our prophetic insight.*

1. Divide into groups of three and have the youngest person share a favorite fragrance. Let the other two members of the group prophesy concerning the meaning of this favorite fragrance.

2. Now have the person to the left share a favorite fragrance and continue the same exercise until everyone has received a prophetic word.

3. For individual activation, ask the Lord, "What is my fragrance to You?" Write down the impressions the Lord gives you in this area.

 ## 14 Favorite Line Prophecy

*Just like we use Scripture and our own creative writing as a trigger for prophetic ministry, we can also use what others have written. Often, a catalyst for a prophetic word can come from a line of a song, or a line from a book, or the dialogue of a movie.*

*Sometimes, when God is speaking, you will hear a song in your head or see a short clip from a movie run through your imagination. I have learned that God really loves to speak through story and song. God is both timeless and contemporary. He is even up on movies, books, and songs from today's market.*

1. Divide into groups of two or three. Ask the Lord to give you quotes from poems, books, songs, or movies for each other. Confirm this leading in your heart with the Lord, and then share with the other person what you are hearing from God.

2. For individual activation, ask the Lord what He is speaking over you personally. Let Him sing a song over you, or, He may even quote a line from your favorite movie.

 ## 15 Finding Your Mountain of Influence

*With this exercise, determine which of the seven mountains is your strongest sphere of influence by taking time to answer these five questions. The seven mountains are: Family, Religion, Business, Government, Education, Arts and Entertainment, and Media. (See Chapter 10 for further explanation of these seven mountains.)*

1. In what area have I seen the greatest amount of influence, favor and authority?

2. In what areas do the task, results, and promotion come most easily to me?

3. Where have I seen the most success with the least amount of effort?

4. In what area am I motivated to work hard and persevere in?

5. In what area do people most positively respond to my gift or input?

If these questions are difficult to answer on your own, pair up with a close friend, family member or leader who knows you well. Sometimes others can spot our graces and giftings better than we can.

## 16 Healing Through Prophetic Acts

*As in the biblical example found in 2 Kings 13, this exercise must be performed with faith and definite passion. Focus on the center of the prayer target's pain. Remember to ask the Lord for sight or perception of where the pain is focused.*

1. Ask your group how many of them have shoulder, back, or neck pain that has no apparent cause. Find out how many of them feel the cause could be a dart or arrow of the enemy. Have those persons come forward and form a line across the front of the room.

2. Ask for volunteers from your group to come up, and with a prophetic action, remove the arrows. Remind them to firmly take hold of the invisible arrow and give it a strong yank.

3. After performing this prophetic act, ask those who had the pain if they notice any change. Some should feel an immediate difference in their pain level; others may have a more natural root or a need that requires another approach to see their full healing.

4. Celebrate all those who are healed, and thank the Lord.

## 17 Healing Words

*Ask the Lord to manifest words of knowledge for healing in your group. Encourage everyone to be sensitive to sympathetic pains within their own bodies or impressions of what the Lord is focusing on for healing.*

1. Have each member of the group share any words of knowledge they are getting for physical healing.

2. Ask those who responded with the condition that was called—or they need healing in that area—to stand up.

3. Have the group member who received the word of knowledge minister healing to those who have stood.

4. Command the pain or condition to go, and release the healing virtue of God.

5. After praying for the person to be healed, ask if there is a change in their condition.

6. Give time for some testimonies of healing at the end of the ministry.

# 18 How God Touched Me

*Before you do this exercise, help the group become aware of the many ways they may experience God's touch. Explain that as they sense the Spirit of God, they might feel a change in a certain part of their body. For instance, their breathing or their mind may come to a state of rest or heightened awareness. Some may feel heaviness, fire or a burning sensation, a tingling, a peace, or the literal touch of a hand.*

1. Have the group close their eyes and be still before the Lord.

2. Pray over the members of the group that God would touch them in a tangible way.

3. Have the members of the group journal how God touched them.

4. Have the group dialogue with the Holy Spirit on what it might mean.

# 19 In-House Treasure Hunt

*If your group is big enough, you can do an in-house treasure hunt. This activation needs sufficient time for everyone to search for the "treasure" in the room or on campus.*

1. Without looking around the room, ask God to show you factors that describe a person (i.e., a name, clothing color, and prayer needs). Write your clues down on a piece of paper. This will be your "treasure map."

2. Release the group to go find the people in the room who match the clues on their treasure maps.

3. When you find the person who matches your clues, show them what was written down and offer to pray for them.

4. After sufficient time, ask how many found someone who matched their clues. Allow some time for testimonies of healing or other significant encounters that happened during the treasure hunt.

5. If there are any participants who did not find the one who matched their clues, encourage them to be watching for that person throughout the rest of the day.

# 20 Internal Triggers

*In this activation divide the group into pairs. Instead of activating with external objects alone, you will use your inner eyesight or sanctified imagination.*

*Remember, each word should be according to our prophetic protocol— encouraging, strengthening, or comforting.*

1. Close your eyes for just a moment and ask the Lord for a picture for the other person. Do you see a still picture, a movie, a flash of color?

2. Share what you see for the other person and what you think it means.

## 21 MAP (Ministry Action Plan)

*You can create a MAP for each of the major promises the Lord has given you with this exercise.*

1. List one of the primary promises God has made concerning you.

2. Under that promise, list the potential areas you will need to develop in order to embrace or sustain that level of promise. Consider areas of personal and character development, resource and financial development, strategic partnership and team development, skills development and spiritual development.

3. Write short goals or targets for each area of development that become the MAP to your promise.

## 22 Most Common Name

*This activation helps prepare you to receive revelation surrounding the most common names. Wikipedia, the free online encyclopedia, lists the most popular given names for every country of the world. In the United States, the top boys' names in 2011 were: Jacob, Mason, William, Jayden, Noah, Michael, Ethan, Alexander, Aiden, Daniel. The most common girls' names were: Sophia, Isabella, Emma, Olivia, Ava, Emily, Abigail, Madison, Mia, Chloe.*[45]

*Feel free to use a different list of common names related to your geographic region.*

1. Write each one of these popular names on a separate 3x5 index card with a dark marker pen.

2. Place the cards in a hat and have volunteers draw from it. The person reads the selected name and then has 30 seconds to deliver a prophetic word related to that name.

3. For individual activation, use the index cards like flash cards, giving different prophetic words related to each name.

## 23 Name that Tune

1. Have each person in the group pair up with another member. If that person were a song, what would the song be and why?

2. Circulate around the room pairing up with others in the same manner. Continue to move about the room until each person has shared a song with at least three other persons.

3. For individual activation, choose three family members. Ask the Lord for a song that represents each one prophetically. Write down the song and any additional reasoning or revelation you receive.

---

45   www.ssa.gov/oact/babynames/

Share it with your family member through a letter, email, or in person.

## 24 National Treasure Hunt

*Have a detailed world atlas and Wi-Fi access available for this exercise.*

1. Have group members ask the Lord for the name of a city, region, or nation. Ask God what the prayer needs are in that location. Write down your clues.

2. Research to find where the location is and how the clues you received might match any news events posted on the internet.

3. Pray and declare the clues you have gathered over that place.

## 25 No Christianese Please

*This activation is great practice for sharing prophetic words on the streets.*

*With this exercise, practice sharing prophetic words without using our Christian subculture language or jargon that a pre-Christian would not understand.*

1. Have your group suggest phrases that Christians often use but that an unbeliever may not understand.

2. Write these words on a whiteboard, chalkboard or large pad of paper.

3. Now ask two volunteers to come to the front of the room. The first volunteer will prophesy over the other without using any of the Christianese words written on the board. This is harder than you may think.

4. Let several volunteers try prophesying without using Christian jargon. You may want to use a buzzer, bell, or a cell phone tone to warn the person when they have used a word from the forbidden list. (This is like the game Taboo.)

5. For individual activation, make a photocopy of prophetic words that you have received. Read through the words and highlight any phrases that use Christianese or Christian jargon phrases. Rewrite the phrases using words that a pre-Christian would understand without significantly altering the meaning. In this way you can practice your vocabulary for prophetic evangelism.

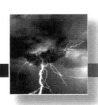

## 26 Pay the Way

*If we watch and prepare for prophetic opportunities, we will see a huge increase in divine appointments and supernatural assignments. A fun way to practice prophetic giving is to make a habit out of paying the way for others.*

*Here are a few ideas.*

1. Plan to pay the way of the car behind you at the toll booth.

2. Pay for the groceries of a young mother or a widow at the store.

3. Purchase tickets for the person behind you in line at the movie theater.

4. Buy an extra grocery item to give away.

5. Place folded dollar bills between jars of baby food in the baby food aisle at the grocery store.

## 27 Personal Treasure Hunt

*Each day can be an adventure in prophetic evangelism. You can do personal treasure hunts on your own to increase the number of divine appointments in your daily routine.*

1. During your morning devotional time, write out several clues of peoples' names, clothing, appearance, and prayer needs that come to mind.

2. Watch and pray for these ministry opportunities to appear during your daily routine at work, school or around the neighborhood.

## 28 Phone-A-Friend Prophecy

*Make this exercise a regular practice of sending prophetic words and encouragement to friends and family through email, social networks, and cell phone text messages.*

1. Choose someone to prophesy over from your cell phone contacts, social network, or email contacts list.

2. Compose a prophetic message in the form of a cell phone text or email message. Because this form of communication is characteristically short, condense your prophetic words down to as few lines as possible. You can start the message with something

like, "I was thinking of you today and felt like I heard…"

3.  Prayerfully send the message.

# 29  Popcorn Prophecy

*This activation trains you in speed, listening and interacting with one another by saying something meaningful in a very short and concise way.*

*One person after another "pops off" a prophetic sentence that relates to that person seated and relates to what was said by the one who spoke just before.*

1.  Find a volunteer and seat them in a chair placed in the middle of a circle. The rest of the group will stand around the person seated.

2.  Each person in the group will speak only one sentence of prophetic encouragement to the one in the middle. Do not share a second pop-prophecy word until each member has spoken.

3.  Keep this prophetic flow going by tagging onto the previous comment in rapid succession.

# 30  Postcard Prophecy

*Have the people in your group bring six to ten postcards or small art prints of various subjects. This exercise will activate prophetic words from these visual clues.*

1. Select a volunteer from the group to choose the photo they are most drawn to.

2. Ask the group to share prophetic encouragements for that volunteer based on the selected photo.

3. Follow this pattern a more few times with different volunteers, each one selecting a card and the rest of the group giving prophetic feedback.

4. Then ask each person in the group to choose one of the cards and journal a personal prophetic word based on the photo they have chosen.

5. For individual activation, choose a piece of artwork in your home, a picture from a magazine, or an advertisement in the mail and journal what the Lord is speaking through that picture.

 31 **Prayer for the Nations**

*Ask the Lord how He would like you to intercede for a specific city or nation. After responding to the Lord's leading through prophetic actions, make sure to track any changes that appear in the nation by watching the media over the coming days. Often there will be direct correlations to specific things you prayed during these times of prophetic actions and intercession.*

*Here are some simple suggestions to get you started in praying for cities and nations:*

1. Lay hands on a map.

2. Aim your arms in a specific direction.

3. Perform a prayer walk or prayer march.

4. Make movements to a song from that specific nation.

## 32 Prophetic Geographic Collage

*This collage poster makes another great prayer tool to remind you to partner with what God is speaking over specific geographical regions.*

1. Gather stacks of old magazines that you can cut up for this project.

2. Have your group scan through the various advertisements and pictures in the magazines looking for words and images that you sense God is speaking over a specific geographic area, i.e., a city, your region, or a nation.

3. Paste the words and images onto a poster board to make a visual statement of what God is speaking about that geographical region.

## 33 Prophetic Collage or Family Crest

*For this exercise, gather stacks of old magazines that can be cut up. Use your "prophetic identity statement"[46]to create a prophetic collage or family crest.*

---

46    See "Prophetic Identity Statement Worksheet" in the Appendix of Prophetic Activations Worksheets.

1. Cut out pictures and words that relate directly to your prophetic identity and paste them into a collage.

2. For a family crest, you may want to choose the 3-4 dominant thoughts from your prophetic identity statement and find an image that represents each one.

3. Paste these images onto a shield or crest shape along with a strategic phrase or two.

## 34 Prophetic Gift Exchange

*This activation trains you to see the prophetic meaning behind a gift.*

1. Print the names of your group members on cards or small slips of paper.

2. Pass out the name cards to each member of the group.

3. Have your group members return the following week with an item from home or something inexpensive purchased at the store that prophetically represents something they feel the Lord is speaking into the life of the person whose name they received.

4. Gather your group in a circle and have them present their gifts one-by-one along with what the Lord is saying through that gift.

## 35 Prophetic Gifts

*This exercise activated by a small prophetic gift can make a great impact on the one receiving it.*

1. Prepare a small gift for a friend or family member that is a trigger for a prophetic encouragement.

2. Write out the word or share it with the person as you give the gift.

 ## 36 Prophetic Identity Statement

*A prophetic identity statement is a written declaration of who God says you are based on the words and phrases He uses to describe you within your personal prophecies. This exercise will be useful for other activations. Use the "Prophetic Identity Statement Worksheet" in the Appendix of Prophetic Activation Worksheets to complete this activation.*

1. Using the circled words from your prophetic processing exercise,[47] make a list of the descriptive phrases embedded in your prophetic words that speak to your identity.

2. From this list of phrases, compose a short biographical paragraph of three to five sentences that describe who God says that you are. Start your paragraph with the statement, "I am..."

3. Once everyone has composed their prophetic identity statements, have them read the statement before the rest of the group.

4. Practice relating to one another according to the way God describes each person. Hold one another accountable to living as the people God says you are.

---

47    See "Processing a Prophetic Word" in Chapter 12.

5. For individual activation, determine to align your character, thoughts, and behavior with the truth of who God says you are. What changes in thought patterns or behaviors will you need to make? Rehearse your prophetic identity statement until you have memorized it and it becomes imbedded in your spirit.

## 37 Prophetic Movements

*Worship times provide another great opportunity to explore the power of prophetic actions.*

1. Turn the lights low in the room so that people will be less self-conscious.

2. Play music that has a prophetic or intercessory tone from a public sound system or portable music player.

3. Invite group members to respond physically to the music without singing. Some may want to dance, march, lift their arms, or bow down.

4. Each group member should practice being sensitive to the Spirit and gain confidence in communicating faith and obedience to the Lord.

## 38 Prophetic Name Badges I

*Make it a habit to practice prophecy that is triggered by names wherever people wear name tags. You can also ask the Lord about those you deal with in the business world and marketplace on a regular basis. In this way, you can regularly arm and prepare yourself for prophetic activation.*

1. If you are in a group that can travel, go on a field trip to places where people wear name tags: markets, banks, restaurants, etc.

2. Look for people who are not busy with customers or their work. Prophesy over that person with a short word of encouragement related to their name.

3. For individual activation, think of people who regularly wait on you at the bank, the grocery store checkout, a favorite restaurant waiter. Ask the Lord for prophetic insights that relate to their names. Print out the results you get and be prepared to share it the next time you see these persons.

# 39  Prophetic Name Badges II

*Here is an exercise based on another skill we learned in Chapter One, "What's in a Name." This activation is designed particularly for teams of people.*

1. Send teams to places where people normally wear name badges, i.e., a restaurant, grocery store, bank, or a local convenience store.

2. At an appropriate time, take a quick moment to share a prophetic word based on the worker's name.

3. If you are sitting in a restaurant, order something to eat. Share your prophetic word with the waiter as the opportunity arises. Make sure to leave a big tip!

4. It is really important to keep your prophetic ministry very brief so as not to keep the employee from his work responsibilities.

# 40 Prophetic Name Game

*This is an activation where the name of a person gives prophetic clues.*

1. If you are in a group, divide into smaller groups of two or three. Prophesy over each other using one of the three name methods[48] as a trigger for prophetic encouragement.

    A. Meaning of names

    B. Famous characters

    C. Sounds similar

2. For individual activation, write a letter or send an email or cell phone text to a friend crafting a prophetic encouragement based upon his or her name.

# 41 Prophetic Sowing

*Identify a dream or vision that you have for your future. Perhaps you are hoping to start a business, buy a home, or go on vacation. It could be a relational dream you have had, like finding a mate or having a child. It could also be a mission-focused dream of starting an orphanage, a non-profit organization, or ministering in another country. See how God would have you give a financial gift as an opportunity to prophetically sow into your own dream or vision.*

---

48    Refer to Chapter One "What's in a Name" for a review of these methods.

1. Write down your dream or vision. If you have more than one of these types of dreams or visions, then write three to five of the most prominent on a piece of paper or in a journal.

2. Pray about how God might have you sow a gift into someone who is doing something similar to your own dream.

3. Pray over the gift or the amount, and tell the Lord that you are joyfully planting this as a seed, prayerfully expecting a harvest from God's goodness. You may want to put more than one seed in the ground.

 ## 42 Prophetic Training Journal

*Once you have determined your primary mountain of influence, you are ready to begin a prophetic training journal.*

*Select a dedicated notebook or journal for this exercise because you will use it for at least one year. This exercise will make a way for you to train yourself in godliness for the mountain of influence that God has given you.*

1. Prayerfully select an influential prayer target from your mountain of influence. For instance, if your mountain is government, you will probably want to choose a national, state, or local leader as your target. If your mountain is family, you could choose a family in your church, an extended family member, or even the marriage of a public figure or celebrity. If your mountain is education, you could choose a local teacher or national scientist or professor.

2. Once you have chosen your primary prayer target, ask the Lord for specific information regarding this person. Ask Him for Scriptures, prophetic promises, promotions, and/or challenges that your

target person will face. Important Note: In this exercise, you will never share these things with the person you are focused on. This activation is still part of your training program. You are training in the secret place for what you believe will happen in the future.

3. Journal all of the clues, proclamations, promises, and prayers that you receive for your target person. In your journal, put a date by all of the prophetic information and activations that you do on your target's behalf. Over the coming days, pay attention to the news media for reports that validate or confirm the information you were getting from God regarding this person.

4. Keep prophesying, tracking your accuracy, and measuring the affect of your expressed blessings in the life of your target without ever establishing communication with the person.

5. Once you have built your faith muscle, skill level, clarity and confidence in the secret place, you will be ready to be a strong prophetic source of encouragement in the future.

# 43 Psalm 23 Prophecy

*This is a great practice for every believer to use during devotional times, not only to feed yourself through the Word and prayer, but also to "pack a lunch" for others. As you are quietly before the Lord, write down Scriptures that stir your heart as they may be for someone else you meet or talk with during the day. Look for opportunities to share the Scriptures you have written down, memorized, or meditated upon. Always have a word like this on your heart, and you will greatly increase the number of divine appointments in your daily life.*

*For this exercise, have each person read Psalm 23.*

1.  Divide the group into pairs.

2.  Each person in the pair will look over Psalm 23 and choose one verse or phrase that stands out to him in that moment. The chosen verses will become the foundation for prophetic encouragements given to each other. For instance, you might start with the verse, "He anoints my head with oil," and then say, "I see the Lord giving you a fresh anointing...it may also involve promotion in a specific area." Here's another example: "He makes me lie down in green pastures and leads me beside the still waters." You could then encourage the person with something like, "I see a season of rest and refreshing for you. God is calming the waters surrounding you and leading you into rest and stillness. In that place you will find fresh revelation and new purpose to your doing."

3.  Remember, in this exercise, use only one line of the Psalm as a prophetic trigger to speak over your partner.

4.  For individual activation, choose the scriptural phrase that really stands out to you and ask the Lord what He is saying to you from that verse. In a journal, write down what Lord is speaking to you.

 ## 44 Secret Friend Prophetic Letter

*Set up this activation by explaining that each person will write out a prophetic word. They do not know for whom they are writing, but God knows. Therefore, they can trust that the word will be led of the Spirit. In actuality, the prophetic word is being written for themselves.*

*This activation reveals that not only can we hear from God to prophesy over others, but God can also speak to us significantly and prophetically about our own identity, destiny and current situations.*

1.  Give everyone about ten minutes to pray and write out the mystery prophetic word.

2.  After the time is up, announce to everyone that the mystery prophetic word they received is actually for themselves personally!

3.  This is a great exercise to activate on your own as often as possible. Allow God to encourage you personally in this way, and you will have something significant to share with someone He sends into your life.

# 45  See the Needs

*Remember that a gift does not always have to be monetary or expensive to make a powerful impact.*

1.  Write down a list of people with whom you regularly interact and consider their specific needs.

2.  Pray over the list and ask the Lord if He would like you to give anything towards one of these needs.

# 46  Sensitivity Journal

*This exercise is designed to build your sensitivity muscle for operating your senses in a Kingdom capacity. The five physical senses are touch, taste, smell, sight, and sound.*

1. During your times of personal devotional worship and prayer, journal the different sensations you experience and how they impacted you.

2. Keep track also of the various ways you encountered God through your senses as you went about your regular daily routine.

# 47 Set a Date

*The truth is, with our busy lives, we often do not remember to pray for our own city, region, or nation. If we don't set an occasion for prayer, then we tend to only pray occasionally. Create an action plan for when you will pray, give thanks and prophesy over your city, region, or nation. I used to call mine "Around the World Wednesdays." On Wednesday mornings I would gather with some friends, and we would pray over and speak to the nations that were upon our hearts.*

1. I recommend that you set a daily, weekly, or monthly appointment for this exercise.

2. Journal what and when you prayed and prophesied so that you can track the accuracy and fulfillments.

# 48 Seven Mountain Prophetic Groups

*Once you have identified the primary mountains of influence within your group, gather in small groups that represent the interest of each mountain of society.*

1. Have each group pray for prophetic information regarding their specific mountain of influence.

2. Compare, clarify, and confirm what each group member is hearing by sharing what you are receiving with others.

3. Take time to declare together the prophetic directions that resonate in the strongest way with your group.

# 49  Show and tell

*In this activation, ask group members to deliver a short prophetic message to one another that includes a prophetic action. This is a great way to practice sharing a message that has a prophetic picture or action associated with it.*

1. For this exercise, you are not allowed to touch the other person or ask the other person to perform any movement or task. The prophetic action or movement will be on the part of the one delivering the word, not the one receiving it. For example, you might stand behind a person with your arms to either side of them like a shield and quote aloud Psalm 3:3, "But you are a shield around me, O LORD; you bestow glory on me and lift up my head."

2. The verbal portion of the prophetic word you deliver should be very short and the action non-intrusive.

# 50  Social Networks and Words of Knowledge

*In the same way that you receive words of knowledge for healing and treasure hunts, you can use emails, cell phone texts, or social network sites to practice words of knowledge.*

*Ask the Lord how you can minister to a friend in need today.*

1. What names, faces, or places come before you?

2. What are the needs?

3. How can you minister to them?

4. With what God gives you, create a cell phone text, email, or social network posting to share this encouragement with your friends.

 ## 51 Spiritual Caller ID

*This is a fun way to practice the word of knowledge and exercise your faith at home.*

1. When the home phone or cell phone rings, try to predict who it is and what the caller wants. Use your "internal caller ID" and practice this until it becomes common to receive the correct information.

2. You can do the same thing when there is a knock at your door. Expect that God will show you who is there through exercising a word of knowledge.

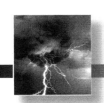 ## 52 Surname Sounds-Like

*Surname is another term for your last name or family name. In this activation group members will use the sounds-like exercise to prophesy over surnames.*

*For example, my last name is McCollam. It sounds like "call 'em." So, someone might prophesy over me about calling in leaders or calling in the lost.*

*In another example, you are talking to a person who has Smith as a surname. You could prophesy about him being a craftsman with words or details, or being sharpened by the Lord.*

1. Have several volunteers stand before your group and share their last names one at a time.

2. Allow volunteers who are seated to give short prophetic encouragements using this sounds-like exercise.

3. After a few words have been given, move on to the next volunteer. Continue on until the group has practiced on several volunteers.

4. For individual activation, use the last names of your three closest friends. Write out prophetic encouragement based on this sounds-like exercise for each of these friends. Be prepared to share it with them at an appropriate time.

 ## 53 Table of Triggers

*For a small to medium-sized group, bring five or six various and seemingly "random" items to trigger prophetic encouragements. Place all items on a table in front of the group.*

1. Have one volunteer from the group choose an item off of the table.

2. Have two or three other volunteers from the group share an encouraging prophetic word with the person who chose the item, using that item as a trigger from which to prophesy.

3. After the prophetic words about that person from the specific

trigger item have been shared, select a new volunteer. The new volunteer may choose any item on the table, including the one that was just recently selected.

4. Get three new volunteers to give a prophetic word triggered from that item.

# 54 The Envelope Please

*This activation is for those who are well-exercised in receiving a word of knowledge, but it is good practice for the inexperienced as well.*

1. From the internet, print off ten photographs of celebrities that everyone in your group would know. These might include politicians, actors, musicians, or religious figures.

2. Place each picture inside an envelope. Then seal the envelopes and give each one a number from 1-10.

3. Have each member of your group take out a sheet of paper and number it 1-10. Leave approximately three empty lines between each number to include additional information.

4. Pass these sealed and numbered envelopes around the group. Without looking inside, each group member will try to get a name, a gender, a hair color, a clothing item or other significant fact about the person whose photo is inside of the sealed envelope. Write up to three clues for each envelope.

5. When everyone has received all ten envelopes and has written down clues for each, open the envelopes and reveal the pictures.

6. Have group members check how many details they got correct concerning the celebrity inside the envelope.

7. For individual activation, ask a friend or family member to prepare the photos and envelopes for you.

Don't be discouraged if you do not get many correct at first, as this is one of the more advanced activation exercises.

 ## 55 The Sounds of Nations

*This is a great activation to pray over specific regions or nations.*

1. Collect ethnic music off the internet from various nations where you have mission interests.[49]

2. Play a single song from each nation and ask friends in your group to craft a prophetic word, picture, image, or sense of what the Lord is speaking over that nation.

3. Move from song to song until all the nations you are focusing on have been covered.

4. After the song time, have everyone stand and declare prophetic words over the nations.

 ## 56 Thirty-Second Drill

*This activation exercises our ability to prophesy quickly and briefly so that we are always prepared to give an encouraging word.*

---

49  See our Sounds of the Nations recordings on iTunes.

1. Number your group 1-2-1-2-1-2, etc., until everyone has received a number.

2. Have the group stand. Announce that in a moment the signal will be given and those with the number one will have 30 seconds to prophesy over the number two on their right. (The persons on the end of the row may need to cross the room.)

3. Give the signal, "Go!" Watch the clock and announce when there are only ten seconds left.

4. At the 30-second mark, call "Stop!"

5. Now with no delay, announce that the twos will also have 30 seconds to prophesy over the number ones on their right. This is a different person than the one who just prophesied over them. Call "Go!"

6. Give the warning when ten seconds remain. After 30 seconds are up, call "Stop!"

7. Now have the number ones prophesy to a number two directly behind them. (Back rows can move to prophesy over the twos in the front row.)

8. Keep using different configurations of the ones and twos until every person has had several opportunities using the thirty-second drill.

## 57 Treasure Hunts

*Kevin Dedmon, one of the pastors at Bethel Church in Redding, California, has made famous the concept of using words of knowledge for evangelistic treasure hunts.*[50] *Many people have been saved, healed, or greatly touched by God's love through this kind of compassionate prophetic evangelism.*

1. In a group of three to five people, ask God for words of knowledge that give specifics about people's names, clothing, appearance, and prayer needs. Also, ask God for words of knowledge about locations and other unusual things.

2. Write these clues down on a paper. This is your "treasure map."

3. The team will travel to the location on the map to find these "treasures" of people according to the specific clues received.

4. When the person who fits the clues is found, show this person the treasure map.

5. Ask the person if they would like prayer for the specific need.

6. For individual activation, see #27 "Personal Treasure Hunt" here in the Appendix of Prophetic Activations.

# 58 What Color Do You See?

*A simple exercise we often use when training children in the prophetic is to ask the question, "What color do you see?"*

1. Divide into pairs.

2. Have each person share what color he sees or perceives on, over, or around the other person.

---

50  *The Ultimate Treasure Hunt* by Kevin Dedmon explains this concept fully.

3. With adults doing this exercise, take the perception further and have them explain why they believe they are seeing that particular color and what it might mean.

4. For those doing these activations on your own, target three leaders in your life with the same question, "What color do you see?"

5. What color do you see on or over your pastor?

6. How about an employer, teacher or adult leader?

7. You can also choose a family member and try to determine what color you see on, over, or around them.

8. Journal these perceptions and watch to see if God provides an opportunity in the future where you could share these insights in an encouraging way.

 59 **What Flavor are You?**

*This exercise is much like "What Color Do you See?" You may experience a literal taste that comes into your mouth or a perceived taste in your imagination as a spiritual impression.*

1. Divide the group into pairs.

2. Ask for a perception of flavor concerning the other person. Share a prophetic word that is triggered by the perception of flavor.

3. Another way to do this exercise is to ask the Lord, "What flavor is this day?" Dialogue with the Lord for an impression of flavor for this day and why.

4. Journal your perceptions at the beginning of the day and do a follow-up entry at the end of the day for how it matched or did not match those perceptions.

# 60 White Elephant Prophetic Gift Exchange

*Plan a "white elephant" prophetic gift exchange with some friends or family members.*

1. Each person participating buys or brings a small gift from home with a prophetic word they received written down and attached to it.

2. Wrap the gifts so that no one knows what they are.

3. Each person in attendance chooses a gift from the table, opens it and reads out loud the prophetic encouragement accompanying the gift.

# 61 Word of Knowledge Journal

*Every day can be a personal treasure hunt. In your devotional time, journal simple things that you expect will happen during the day.*

1. Who will you meet?

2. Who will call?

3. What things will happen?

4. What are the needs you must be prepared to meet today?

5. Ask yourself: What Scriptures or encouragements have I recently received that I can have on hand to minister to the needs of others?

Write down your clues or expectations for the day and journal the results before bed or sometime the following day.

Mobilizing a prophetic
word is about living as
the person Heaven says
you are.

# Prophetic Identity Statement Worksheet

*This worksheet will help to determine your*
*personal identity through Heaven's eyes.*

1. Gather several personal prophesies that resonate with you. Type them out double-spaced. Circle all the words in your personal prophecy that describe who you are. List those descriptive words or phrases below.

_____    _____

_____    _____

_____    _____

_____    _____

2. From this list of phrases, compose a short biographical paragraph of three to five sentences that describe who God says you are. Start each sentence with the statement, "I am . . ."

I am _____

_____

I am _____

_____

I am _____

_____

I am _____

_____

I am _____

# Processing a Prophetic Word

*This worksheet is designed to help process your prophetic words and put them into active service.*

1. Write out the prophetic word you want to process.

2. Circle any words that refer to who God says you are. We call these "identity words."

3. Underline any promises God is making directly to you.

4. Write out any conditions or requirements the prophetic word is asking you to fulfill.

_____

_____

5. List any words that indicate timing or seasons.

_____

_____

6. Make a list of any metaphors or biblical references that you want to research further.

_____

_____

_____

7. Notice how many times a word, idea, or theme is repeated. Repetition is a clue to major and minor themes within your prophetic words. What themes do you see?

_____

_____

# About the Author

Dan McCollam travels internationally as a prophetic speaker and trainer. He strategizes with churches and individuals to create prophetic cultures in which everyone can hear God, activate and mobilize their prophetic words, and express their own unique prophetic diversity.

Dan has developed many resources that offer a fresh perspective on the prophetic, supernatural Kingdom life, biblical character and spiritual gifting. He is well-known as a great friend of the Holy Spirit and one who carries and imparts wisdom, revelation, and breakthrough.

Dan serves on the teaching faculty of Bethel School of the Prophets and the School of Worship in Redding, California. He is part of the Global Legacy apostolic team that oversees a growing number of churches in partnership for revival. He serves on the core leadership team at his home church, The Mission, in Vacaville, California, with his wife Regina, and is a director of Deeper School of Supernatural Life also in Vacaville.

# Sounds of the Nations and iWar

After serving as a worship leader for 20 years and releasing Kingdom worshipers locally, regionally, and globally on countless mission trips to nations around the world, Dan became troubled over the westernization of worship in the majority of churches in which he ministered. Indigenous sounds had often been labeled sinful by church leadership. Since the sounds of every tribe and nation are heard in Heaven, becoming an agent in restoring the stolen authentic expressions of worship became a driving passion for Dan, and Sounds of the Nations was born.

As international director of Sounds of the Nations and the Institute for Worship Arts Resources (iWar), Dan trains indigenous peoples to write and record worship songs using their own ethnic sounds, styles, languages, and instruments.

# More Books by Dan McCollam

## Finding Your Song
**Dan McCollam**

Featuring songs by Brian and Jenn Johnson

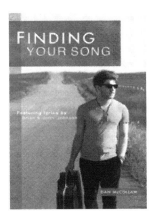

*Finding Your Song* explores seven sources of inspiration for writing great praise and worship songs. Working examples are taken from the writings of **Brian and Jenn Johnson** along with quotes from some of the greatest worship writers of our day.

**Available for sale at iBethel.org/store and tmvvstore.org**

Book : $10

---

## The Worship Writer's Guide
**Dan McCollam**

Fourteen lyrical and melodic tools for crafting excellent praise and worship songs.

Creativity is not just inspiration; it also has its deep roots in wisdom, knowledge, and understanding. *The Worship Writer's Guide* is designed to give you the song craft tools that are based on the timeless principles of great songwriting.

**Available for sale at iBethel.org/store and tmvvstore.org**

Book : $10

# For more resources from Dan McCollam,

visit iBethel.org/store or tmvvstore.org

online stores and search for

## "Dan McCollam" or "Sounds of the Nations."

Original worship music from

## Sounds of the Nations

is also available on

## iTunes.

---

## Understanding Your Metron
**Dan McCollam**

Explore the demographic and geographic spheres of influence where your prophetic gift has the greatest authority, influence and favor.

**Available Options:**

Audio CD : $10          MP3 Download : $4

# Encouragement
## Dan McCollam

Many people feel that correction or judgment is a higher level of prophetic operation. This message reveals the true expressions of prophetic maturity. Encouragement is the mother tongue of the Holy Spirit.

**Available Options:**

Audio CD (1) : $10          MP3 Download:  $4

---

# Anachronistic Living:
## Pulling Future Prophetic Promise into Present Reality

## Dan McCollam

In this message from The Prophetic Series, you will discover the principles of how to live powerfully and practically in the present while possessing a prophetic vision for a more desirable future.

**Available Options:**

Audio CD (1)  : $10          MP3 Download:  $4

# Prophetic Culture and Identity
## Dan McCollam

Prophetic Culture and identity is a two-part series. In this series, you will be taken on a journey to discover the ingredients for creating prophetic culture. Then learn the craft of defining yourself by how heaven sees you.

**Available Options:**

Audio CD (1) : $10          MP3 Download: $4

---

# Living on the Right Side of the Cross
## EXTENDED VERSION
## Dan McCollam

The six-session extended version of the popular original release, *Living on the Right Side of the Cross,* is now available.

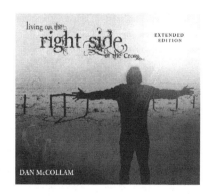

**Session One: The Wrong Side**
Recognize the symptoms of not fully understanding the benefits of the cross.

**Session Two: Getting on the Right Side**
Renew your mind with four power positions vital to living on the right side of the cross.

**Session Three: Dealing with Sin and Temptation**
Unpack practical and theological principles reinforcing your victory over sin.

**Session Four: The Ascended Lifestyle**
Grasp the glories of the present tense realities of the resurrection.

**Session Five: Accessing the Ascended Lifestyle**
Discover two keys to accessing the benefits of living on the right side of the cross.

**Session Six: New Creation Realities**
Say goodbye to the "Adam's Family" and hello to your inheritance in the "last Adam," Jesus Christ.

**Available Options:**   Audio CDs (3) : $25          MP3 Download: $15

68579172R00142

Made in the USA
San Bernardino, CA
06 February 2018